CHRISTIAN FACTS AND FORCES

CHRISTIAN

FACTS AND FORCES

BY

NEWMAN SMYTH

AUTHOR OF "OLD FAITHS IN NEW LIGHT," "THE REALITY OF FAITH," ETC.

*" Who climbs keeps one foot firm on fact
Ere hazarding the next step."*—BROWNING.

WIPF & STOCK · Eugene, Oregon

Wipf and Stock Publishers
199 W 8th Ave, Suite 3
Eugene, OR 97401

Christian Facts and Forces
By Smyth, Newman
Softcover ISBN-13: 978-1-6667-6169-6
Hardcover ISBN-13: 978-1-6667-6170-2
eBook ISBN-13: 978-1-6667-6171-9
Publication date 10/10/2022
Previously published by Charles Scribner's Sons, 1887

This edition is a scanned facsimile of the original edition
published in 1887.

TO CENTER CHURCH

This Sheaf of Sermons,

GATHERED, WITH ONE EXCEPTION, FROM MY LAST YEAR'S MINISTRY,

IS NOW PRESENTED AS A THANKOFFERING,

AND DEDICATED

To the Memory of the Many Friends

WHOM I HAVE SEEN PASS FROM ITS COMMUNION, WHOSE DEAR LIVES

HAVE BEEN THE EVIDENCE OF THOSE VITAL CHRISTIAN

FAITHS WHICH I WOULD CONFESS IN ITS

HISTORIC PULPIT.

CONTENTS.

I.
THE CHANGED WORLD, ... PAGE 1

II.
THE HONESTY OF JESUS, ... 14

III.
STANDING IN THE TRUTH, ... 26

IV.
THE POSITIVENESS OF JESUS, ... 38

V.
THE BEGINNINGS OF DISCIPLESHIP, ... 51

VI.
SIGNS OF THE TIMES, ... 62

VII.
THE NOTE OF UNIVERSALITY, ... 76

VIII.

ZEBEDEE'S ABSENCE, ... 92

IX.

THE CHRISTIAN REVELATION OF LIFE, ... 105

X.

RECONCILIATION WITH LIFE, ... 117

XI.

THE GLORIFICATION OF LIFE, ... 130

XII.

A REAL SENSE OF SIN.—A LENTEN SERMON, ... 144

XIII.

PERSONAL POWER, ... 157

XIV.

THE GREAT REQUIREMENT, ... 170

XV.

MISUNDERSTANDING CHRIST, ... 184

XVI.

PUTTING THE WITNESS AWAY, ... 197

XVII.

A STUDY FOR A DOCTRINE OF THE ATONEMENT, ... 210

XVIII.

PAGE

THE GOSPEL A GIFT TO THE SENSES, ... 225

XIX.

THE LIMITS OF SPIRITUAL MANIFESTATION, ... 240

XX.

THE INTERDEPENDENCE OF ALL SAINTS, ... 254

CHRISTIAN FACTS AND FORCES.

I.

THE CHANGED WORLD.

"And the shepherds returned, glorifying and praising God for all the things that they had heard and seen, even as it was spoken unto them."—LUKE ii. 20.

THE shepherds returned to their customary work in the morning, or some time during the day, after Christ had been born in Bethlehem. And in the course of that day after the nativity, the shepherds' story was made known abroad, and "all they that heard it wondered at those things which were told them by the shepherds."

The day after the hour of Christ's advent was a new day in the history of the world. It was not the same world the day after Christmas that it had been the day before. Something had happened, that holy night at Bethlehem, while men were sleeping, and only a few shepherds were watching, which ushered in a new era in the history of the world. The old passed away, the new era began, and only the angels knew what a revolution had been wrought by the quiet power of God. The wonder of that day after the Advent has grown with the years. Christianity has been an increasing miracle of the Lord's presence on earth. That song which a few shepherds heard, has sung itself into the thought of the world, and is the key-note and harmony of all peace and good-will on earth.

Let us think what a changed world it has become because Jesus was born at Bethlehem.

Remember, first, that the Christian change of the world's history is a fact. It has been accomplished. The shepherds came to Bethlehem, and returned to their flocks, and everything went on with them as before; but in those still hours between two days some unseen Power had descended, and quietly altered the whole course of human history. Each succeeding age increases the effect of that holy hour at Bethlehem. The life which then came into our humanity has been cumulative in its power.

When we speak with men about believing, they will sometimes say, "We cannot walk in the air. We must step to our conclusions upon solid facts. These Christian prospects are devoutly to be desired; but we can go no farther than we can find firm footing from fact to fact of experience." Here, then, is something for us to stand upon which is not as a cloud in the air, but which is a fact of the earth. The world has been changed by that life which was begun in the manger. This changed world is a fact. The new Christian evolution of humanity is a fact. The influx through Christ of a new power into the life of humanity is a known fact of experience, as certain as the fact of the battle of Gettysburg, or the island of St. Helena, or the dawn of day. I may shut my eyes to it, and say, if I wish, "It is nothing to me." But the fact remains that this world was one thing the day before Christmas, and that it was a different world, with a new life in its heart, and a new creative power in its civilization, after Christ had been born in Bethlehem.

This fact of the new power in the world through the birth of Christ, we can see, also, belongs to a series or connection of facts. The religion of the Bible presents a continued succession and reveals an exalted order of facts. It is a history of redemption which confronts us. Christianity is a positive religion of historical facts from Moses to Christ, from Christ to the last church which has been organized, and the last communion-table which has been spread. We may say that we do not understand these events; or we may seek to stretch the laws of nature sufficiently to comprehend these Christian results within the network of physical causes; but, however we may learn to account for them, these effects of Christ upon the world, we must observe, are facts, and constitute an order of facts. In approaching the claims of Jesus Christ upon us we have to do not with a vague philosophy, or a pleasant hope, or some happy dream, but with spiritual facts; and with facts, too, which are become so concrete in the institutions of society, and which are so present and vital in our whole civilization, that it is utterly unscientific and wholly unbecoming a logical mind not to take them into consideration, and to reason from them as facts with at least as much assurance as we feel in dealing with any other class and succession of facts. The fact that Jesus was born, and that his Spirit has changed the world, and is changing it, is a simple, undeniable fact to which every reasonable mind should adjust its working-theory of life.

Let us proceed then to inquire, secondly, concerning the nature and real significance of this fact that the world has been changed since the advent of Christ.

In Christianity we breathe a different air. We live in a new order of society. Midway down the Simplon pass the traveller pauses to read upon a stone by the wayside the single word, "*Italia.*" The Alpine pines cling to the mountain sides between whose steeps the rough way winds. The snows cover the peaks, and the brooks are frozen to the precipices. The traveller wraps his cloak about him against the frost that reigns undisputed upon those ancient thrones of ice-bound rock. But at the point where that stone with the word *Italia* stands, he passes a boundary-line. From there the way begins into another world. Soon every step makes plainer how great has been the change from Switzerland to Italy. The brooks, unbound, leap laughing over the cliffs. The snows have melted from the path. The air grows warm and fragrant. The regiments of hardy pine no longer struggle in broken lines up the mountain side. The leaves of the olive trees glisten in the sunshine. The vines follow the wayside. The sky seems near and kind. And below, embosomed in verdure, Lake Maggiore expands before him. As he rests at evening time he knows that the entrance into a new world was marked by the word *Italia* upon that stone at the summit of the pass. Humanity has crossed a boundary-line between two eras. Up to

Bethlehem was one way, growing bleaker, and more barren, and colder, as man hastened on. Down from Bethlehem has been another and a happier time. The one civilization was as Switzerland shut in among its icy Alps; the other is as Lombardy's fruitful plain. The one led up to Stoicism; the other opens into charity. Judaism, also, and the Gospel are as two different climes. We need deny no pagan virtue, we need exaggerate no pagan vice, in order to bring out the greatness of the change which began at Bethlehem. For it is not simply a difference in men, or in civilizations which we have to observe, great as, without historical exaggeration, that may be shown to be; but the advent of Christ marks a difference in motives, and in the motive-powers, which make human life, and which are creative of civilizations. It was the coming of a new power to change the world. The impulse which was imparted to humanity by the presence among men of Jesus Christ can be compared to nothing less potential than the impulse which was given, we may suppose, to the creation when motion first became a fact and law of primeval matter. And from the advent of motion dates the order of the worlds.

What was this new power which came into this world to bring to pass a new era? To the disciples it was Jesus himself. He was the new Power that made all things new to them. At this distance, and in our familiarity with the completed Gospel, we can hardly understand in what a wonder of life the disciples dwelt in the presence of Christ. The Gospels make little note of the feelings of the disciples, yet over and over again the expression of their wonder occurs: "They were exceedingly amazed;" "They were astonished with a great astonishment;" "And Jesus was going before them: and they were amazed." There are many questions which we think we would at once want to ask of Christ now, should he appear once more among us as of old,—questions of our hearts about the future, concerning the unseen world, and what death really is, and what those many mansions are like, and how there our dear ones are; and we have an immense curiosity sometimes to go ourselves straight beyond death, to lift the veil, and to know the great reality, what it is, which we must believe lies just beyond our sight and touch, the First and Last, the final Truth of things. But the disciples, when Jesus was present with them, seem not to have pressed these questions upon him, but to have followed him wondering in the way; and quietly, surely, even as the coming of the dawn changes the whole face of nature, Jesus' presence changed the world to the disciples' eyes, and with his glory in it, never could it become again the hopeless world that it had been in the days before Christmas morn. The men who had been with Jesus did not live any longer in the Judea of the Israelites, nor did they know longer the Samaria of the Samaritans. Galilee's lake had seen the Son of God walking upon its waves, and the risen Lord had appeared upon its shore. It was not, it could not be, the same world after they had once seen Christ in it. If we could put side by side, and print in parallel columns the thoughts, and wishes, and purposes, of Peter or John, when as young men they went fishing on Galilee, and the thoughts of life and death, of heaven and of God, which St. Peter knew on his way to martyrdom, and St. John received on the island of Patmos, we should have before us in those parallel columns the evidence of as signal a miracle as has been recorded in the Gospels—a greater wonder than the change of water into wine, a sign more significant of divinity than the physical manifestations and incidents of the new power of God in Christ on earth; for it would be the evidence of a mental and moral revolution, of a re-creation of character and a new birth of souls—a marvellous work in the moral sphere revealing the coming of a higher spiritual Power, and the unusual presence of God with man. One cause, and one cause only, measures the vastness of that change in the mental and moral realm: "We beheld his glory, the glory as of the only begotten of the Father, full of grace and truth."

There are two particulars in which we may describe further this change as it lies before us, an actual thing, in history.

First, Jesus has been to the world a new revelation of God. Man has seen God in Christ as man never saw God before. It is fashionable for intellectual men, or rather, I should say—for the fashion of this world's thought changes—a few years ago it used to be in good intellectual form for men to say, "We may believe that God exists, but we cannot know anything of God." That passing fashion of thought, however, was fatally illogical, because the very words which were in vogue in some quarters about God, such as, He is the unknown and unknowable Power, really affirmed something, of which we have some latent idea, about the unknown God. And we may have real, though finite knowledge of infinite things. I can know what light is by a single ray in my eye, although I cannot contain in my eye the infinite flood of light which fills all space. And I may know God by a single beam of truth in my soul, although I cannot know God in his infinitude of being. To us men who are capable, then, of receiving truth from God because we are made in the image of God, Jesus Christ brought a new revelation of the essential and eternal character of God. And what was that revelation? Not an image of deity for the Holy Place of the Temple, in which was no likeness of God. Not a map of the divine attributes, such as are found in the books of the schoolmen. Not a form of God which we may look upon and worship as a picture of divinity in our imaginations. Jesus is never depicted pointing his disciples to the sky, as we do, when we say to our children, God is there, Heaven is up above. You cannot find in the teaching of Jesus one word about God's nature which is addressed to these bodily senses. But when Philip said, "Show us the Father,"—poor bewildered disciple, finding the truth he had been learning too great for him, and thinking, If I could only know the Father, if I could only see God as I see man,— then Jesus said, "Have I been so long time with you, and dost thou not know me, Philip? he that hath seen me hath seen the Father." That was his revelation, his new, world-changing revelation of God. Himself, his Person, his character, his conduct—you know that; such is God. The one word which declares God is Christ. *Christlikeness* is what God is. God is essentially and eternally Christlike.

And is not that a new revelation of God? It is new still, even to some of us, for we have hardly dared, even in our churches, always to think of God as Christlike. It is sometimes new theology for us to think clearly, boldly, gloriously of God as Christlike. We receive that clear, white light from the character of God, and break it into partial colors upon the surfaces of our troubled thoughts. We do not often enough let the simple truth that God is Christlike fall full upon us, and illumine the depths of our souls. We think of God as the Almighty One enthroned above the world; we reason anxiously concerning his government and his decrees; we receive the Roman image of an august Cæsar, and in that imperial mould suffer our idea of Divine sovereignty to take form, when the Gospels present Jesus Christ to us as the express image of God's person. We take texts of Scripture in hard literalness, and draw rigid conclusions about God's eternal purposes, which fall like blows upon tender consciences; men speak with cool confidence about God's dealings with dead heathen, as though one day of nature were enough for the God of grace to give to them, and the Christ, who shall have been preached to every creature, will not sit upon the final judgment-throne; and zealous audiences applaud as though the faith were defended; and all the while there is the Lord Christ of the Scriptures watching us, bearing with our cruel misunderstandings of his Father and ours, and waiting for us to come as little children to learn of him, that he may show us the Father, and give us such loyal confidence in him, that when we cannot understand his judgments, or know the whole counsel of his will, we may refuse, with a great-hearted and noble faith, to think any thought of our God which may seem to cast a shadow upon the infinite Christlikeness of his nature. Martin Luther was a truer Christian and a braver defender of the faith when he exclaimed, with a grand impatience of the Papists who pressed him with proof-texts from the Bible, "I confide in Christ, who is true Lord and Emperor of the Scriptures."

This knowledge of God in Christ, albeit we have not yet begun to receive it as we may, has proved itself to be a re-creative and reorganizing power among men. It is the most practical and potential influence in modern life. Nothing indeed can be more practical than a man's habitual thought of his God. A man's idea of his God is as practical as is the north star. Deception about the star means shipwreck upon the coast. And this revelation of God in Christianity has been the pole-star of modern history. This Christian revelation has been, and is now, the guiding principle, the dominant truth of human life. It were blindness not to see and to follow it.

I can but glance now at the other aspect of Christ's new epoch to which I have just alluded.

Secondly, Christ is also a new revelation of man. As man is discovered to us in Christ, he is found to be a new creature. Man is in Christ another man. It will make a vast difference with us whether we habitually look upon man as created in Christ, or without Christ. You go down the street, and pass some one who is only to you another of the multitude of human beings of whom there seem sometimes to be already many more than there is any use for on this earth. You do not know that man, and do not want to know him. He may be only some worthless creature who hives, with other miserables, in some tenement house which was built by the devil of greed, and has been rented to demons of vice and squalor. Only some Board of Health, or the police, have occasion to know the habitats of so much swarming and festering humanity! Or the man you meet may be respectable and honest enough, for all you know, only he exists, and must live his life, whatever it may be, in some one of those worlds which lie below the one into which you were born, and, properly enough, his name is not to be found written in your book of life.

You owe him, you will admit, "equal rights," "liberty to make contracts," a certain humanity, and, if he ever should happen to come to your church, a seat in somebody else's pew. Something like that, in spirit, was the old-world view of man before Christmas. That is the view of him which you might take had you not been baptized into the name of Christ, in whom our whole common humanity exists, redeemed and capable of a great salvation. When that view of a man as a mere man was generally taken in the days before Christmas, the sun looked down upon this earth and saw Cæsar on his throne, and the slave at his oar in the galley; the plunder of whole provinces grasped by the hand of power, and the Roman proletariat rotting in heaped-up worthlessness; sensuousness filling its poisoned cup full at Pompeii, while Vesuvius was gathering underground its judgment-flames; conjuring priests in the temples laughing behind the altars at their incantations; a few Stoics saying brave, impracticable things, and a whole Roman empire dissolving in the fervent heat of its passions and lusts. But what thought Jesus Christ of humanity as he came from the Father, and met that publican in Jericho? As he went to God what said the Lord Jesus to that thief upon a cross? As Jesus' revelation of God was vivifying, and is potential with blessing for the whole world, so also his revelation of man is wonderfully ennobling and transfiguring. Jesus brought out, perfected, and showed in his own divine person, the true image of humanity. Man is made to become Christlike. Man may be saved to Christlikeness. That commonplace man whom we do not know, that poor man whom we may help, is more to us than merely another human being; he has part with us in the humanity of Jesus Christ. All men, all generations of men, all nations of men, are created in Christ, and belong to that one humanity which Jesus Christ has taken to himself, and whose sin he bore in his own body on the tree. And it makes a vast difference in our thought, and hope for men, whether we look upon men as crowding, millions upon millions of them, within this brief space of existence, and pushed on, generation after generation of them, into the dark abyss of death and oblivion, in which all is over; or whether we look upon them all as the children of God, belonging to that humanity which was created in Christ, and which Christ has redeemed, and, as members of that humanity, having all around them its gracious possibility of eternal life for all who will. And as individuals we have to take our place, and to help others find their place, in this saved humanity, this redeemed society of Jesus Christ. There can be no private salvation for us in Christ. There is no salvation for us as individuals except as we belong to the saved humanity which Jesus is redeeming. This is the larger human truth beneath the old, Catholic idea, that there is no salvation without the Church. This revelation also of man in Christ we are only beginning to understand; but we may be sure that the coming great missionary epoch of the Church will be an era of faith moved, governed, and inspired by a broader, higher, more generous vision both of Christ's revelation of God, and his revelation of man,—the one a manifestation of God in his essential and eternal Christlikeness, and the other a discovery of man in the Christlike possibilities of his being.

But I must break off my sermon with the personal question for each one of us: Am I living, by faith in the Son of God, in the changed world? Is it in the history of my soul the day before, or the better day after Christmas?

II.

THE HONESTY OF JESUS.

"The words that I speak unto you, they are spirit, and they are life."— JOHN vi. 63.

I WISH to speak of a certain quality of the Gospel, of which, it seems to me, the Christian world is gaining a clearer and firmer perception. This peculiar quality of the Gospel I might define as the thorough honesty of the mind that was in Jesus toward the life of the world around him. The teaching of the new prophet from Galilee was honesty itself in comparison with the words of the scribes. And still among all the books that have been written, none has a ring so decidedly clear and genuine as the New Testament. What is there in the whole history of the world so honest as the Sermon on the Mount? Yet honesty is not the whole of this singular and significant quality of the life, teaching, and work of Jesus, which I am seeking to describe. For a man may be quite honest, and yet be greatly mistaken. A man may have an honest heart, and yet by accident of education, or by some perversion of disposition, hold his mind at anything but a right angle toward life; so that in his oblique position toward things very distorted images of them may be reflected in his intellect, and the light which would shine straight into the depth of his soul may be mostly reflected and lost from his thoughts. It is a great thing to have a candid mind, one not obscured by the gathered dust of the years, nor broken by the violence of passion—to have and to keep among men a crystalline soul. But this is not enough. A diamond is dark in a dark place. The position of a mirror in the light, and the angle in which it is held toward the object which is to be seen in it, are quite as important as the clearness of the glass. We cannot hope to gain true representations of life and death, and eternal verities, if we persist in holding ourselves at a wrong personal angle toward truths. It is precisely this quality, over and above common honesty, which attracts and commands us in the record of Jesus Christ. He seems, with instinctive and natural adjustment, always to keep himself in a relation so true to men, women, and things, that in his thoughts and judgments all objects are represented in their simple reality, and we see them just as they are. Hence there is always an impression of reality in the words of Jesus. Not only are they clear, honest words, but they correspond to the truth of things. Jesus' mind mirrors reality. This quality of the Gospel might be called, accordingly, the realism of the Gospel. Yet this word also, as well as the word honesty, fails to bring out fully the truth of Christ and Christianity, which the Spirit is showing to us anew in these days. For not only do the narratives of the New Testament give us honest portraitures, and reproduce with vivid realistic touches the persons who come and go before Jesus, but also Christ's words seem always to reach straight down to the moral substance of things, and his judgments disclose the moral realities which lie beneath all the endless fictitiousness of human life. The moral reality of the universe seems ever to be coming to revelation in the teaching of Jesus. This quality, accordingly, of which I wish to speak, might be expressed, so far as a single phrase can denote it, by the words, the moral realism of Christ and Christianity.

Let me proceed, first, to illustrate and to describe more particularly this preëminent characteristic of the Gospel. You must often have noticed, in reading the New Testament, how Jesus in his conversations with men quietly brushes aside their Jewish notions, or their personal deceptions and touches with his saving power the real lives of people. And when man or woman stood for a moment beneath Jesus' eye, always then the real self was revealed. Men could not help appearing before Jesus as they were. They might have hidden the true self from others, but Jesus saw it at a glance. They might have concealed for years the real self from themselves, as so many are doing in their comfortable, fictitious lives; but when Jesus came nigh them they began to feel as though the judgment day were at hand. Before Jesus, in one word, men and women became real. In his clear presence they knew themselves, and were made known as they were. It was so that night in the quiet conversation upon the housetop beneath the stars, when a Master in Israel discovered that even he must be born again of the Spirit. So by Jacob's well at mid-day, a woman whom disciples looked upon only as a poor Samaritan, and who had sinned and suffered enough to make her life hardly worth living more, discovered that she too had a soul, was not a menial Samaritan, but a woman, who even at her weary task of filling her pitcher at the well might minister to the Lord Christ, and all the way as she came and went, in any place, might worship God in spirit and in truth. So the publican, as wretched an outcast as ever was seen loitering down by the water-side of a city, when the Lord's kind word came in its great surprise to him, discovered that he too was a man for all that, and he might hope to live as a son of God in the kingdom. So the Pharisee stands out in Christ's light, discovered in his blindness of soul and pious hatefulness of heart, judged for all time by Jesus' coming to him. And so also the disciples who followed the Master began to know themselves really and truthfully and hopefully, as they never had seen themselves before.

Again, this same quality pervades the teaching of Jesus. Not only did the Master bring out what was real in men, but also his doctrine is characterized throughout by this same note of moral reality. In other words, there was never a conventional phrase used, never an unreal thing said by our Lord in his personal dealings with men and women. He gave to each soul the bread of life which it needed at the time he met it. Jesus Christ sought to make genuine men—men not sound in word merely, or in profession and creed, but sound at heart—whole men before God. Consequently his words went to the moral core of their being. First, they were to become true men at heart. They must have the right will of life, even as he did the will of the Father. Jesus' word in every instance of his conversation with men and women goes straight to the moral heart of the character. He will not accept any homage, he will not grant any prayer, he will not give his blessing to any disciple, until he is sure that the right will has been born of the Spirit in the inmost soul. That will to do the will of God is the essential faith to which Christ declares himself, and he made every work of healing dependent upon that morally real faith in him. We have read the Gospels to little purpose if we have not discovered this. We may study the doctrines of the church until we say we see, as the Pharisees did, and are willing, as they were, to contend for every iota of our traditions; but we shall be blind to the light which lies upon every page of the Gospel, if we will not perceive that faith in Jesus Christ means moral truth and moral reality at the core of the character and in the substance of the conduct, and that only in thorough-going honesty and moral reality of life can we know the doctrine of the man who has told us the truth which he heard from God.

I have just been remarking that Jesus in his conversations with men brought their real dispositions to the light, and, moreover, that his teaching was intended to put men upon thoroughly honest, morally real courses of life. More than this should now be said of his teaching. His doctrine of God throughout has this same practical relation to human life. The doctrine of Jesus means real righteousness, real justice, real love, one and the same in God and man. The theology of Jesus is real theology. It is the bread of life. It is truth of heaven brought down to immediate human uses. It is truth of God, not to be thought about merely, but to be done on earth. It is the truth of the kingdom of heaven put into parables, so that the people may take it home and live upon it. The Lord Jesus Christ did not come into this world to teach a comprehensive system of philosophy, a subtle science of nature, or some perfect scheme of divinity. He came to seek and to save that which is lost. He came to establish the kingdom of heaven on earth. His words are spirit and life. Such is the theology of Christ—a truth of God indeed, into which the thought of the ages may gaze wondering and worshipping—a glory and a mystery of Godliness which transcends our reason as the heaven is high above the earth—a theology for the intellect which will always yield new answers to old questions, and which no age can exhaust—a revelation of God having for our understandings authority as the truth;—but first and chiefly the theology of Jesus Christ, in its whole scope of doctrine, and in all its revelation of heaven and hell, is a theology for the conduct of life, a teaching from God in which divine truths and spiritual energies are brought into vital contact with the real life of men and women and children. Jesus' doctrine was not indeed first a doctrine about God, but a fact of God with man and for man, even as Jesus himself was not first to his disciples an article in the creed of his church, but a Person real, glorious, transfigured, divine. The Life was the light of men; the light came from the Life; the doctrine of Jesus shone from the life and work of Jesus. That was real as God is real, real as love is real, real as a new inspiration of life is real, as a Christlike spirit is real, as the Power of God transforming character is real in human history. And if we do not understand this, if the Lord Jesus Christ does not come to us in this moral reality of his character, convincing us of sin, with his eye searching what is true or false in us, and his divine manhood commanding us to rise and walk in the power of God; if we do not begin to realize down to the bottom of our souls that the doctrine of Christ means for you and me a real repentance and a real faith which shall eventually make us Christlike as he is Godlike, that we all may be made perfect in one,— then, if we will not so learn Christ, and have the Spirit of Christ, we are in danger of the judgment. If we are resting in any fictions and falsehoods either of empty religious profession or of devouring worldliness, it is true of us that we are making our beds in Hell; and if any of us will go on in lives that are shams, and with souls that are frauds, we ought to be consumed at the last day by that Truth of God which is to everything false a consuming fire. This universe is honest from its foundation-stones up to the throne of God, who made it in truth; and there is no resting-place or final hope for a dishonest man in an honest universe. As we would escape loss of soul in lives that are foolish fictions or wicked lies, we need to go penitently, every one of us, to Him who is the most real man of history, the Man who tells us the truth which he heard from God; we need to let him be Master and Lord to us, and before that commanding Character to be converted, to become as little children, and to take up our lives anew in his name.

I have been speaking of the intense moral realism

of Jesus' teaching. Yet one thing more must be said of it. Jesus not only came as the Teacher sent from God, but also put himself in the Father's place among men. He represented God on earth. And this representation of God in Christ was not something scenic, or forensic, or pictorial merely. Jesus realized on earth what God is in heaven. Jesus made real in his life and death, Jesus *realized* in time and space the whole eternal disposition and love of God toward the world. The Cross of Christ is not only the exhibition, it is the *realization* in the midst of human history of God's mind, and will, and heart, toward the sin of the world.

This truth of Christ as the real presence and power of God in the life of the world, is visibly set before us in the one memorial which Jesus left of his death. He might have bequeathed, to be treasured from age to age with reverent care, a parchment-roll written with his last message and his name; or he might have given a new table of commandments graven on stone. He might have left as his memorial an institute of government, or a form of worship, or a liturgy for humanity's prayer. But he gave as his memorial the broken bread and the fruit of the vine. This also is part of the moral realism of his Gospel. These are the true, vital emblems of what he has done for the life of the world; these are signs and pledges of what Christ is in the characters of men. The Lord's words are still startling in their intense literalism: "He that eateth my flesh, and drinketh my blood." Can we not understand how he would show us that our religion must be a vital principle, that his words, which are spirit and life, must enter into the substance and quality of our souls, as the bread we break becomes the life of the body?

Let me turn now, for a few moments, from this endeavor to describe the thorough honesty, or moral realism of the Gospel, to some pertinent applications of this truth. If we can gain a more thoroughly real conception of what religion is, and what Christ is, we shall understand better how the Spirit of God is now moulding and developing the Christianity of the world. There are two facts which are forcing themselves upon our notice: first, ecclesiastical Christianity, and to some extent dogmatic Christianity, have less influence among men now than they ever have had since Constantine proclaimed an empire to be Christian, or Augustine, and Calvin after him, built and closed the massive Latin theology. We may regret, or not, this fact; but no one who knows men, and the movements of modern life, can ignore the evidence of it. The other present fact is, that never has a morally real Christianity, a Christianity of real life, been more honored, more loved, more believed in among men. It would seem, therefore, to require no prophet to predict that the Church of the future will not be altogether the Church of the past. Indeed, the way of the Spirit of the Lord since Christ ascended has never yet turned wholly back upon itself. It seems clear that the Church of the future is not to be a church of vested ecclesiastical pretension, or of one-sided insistence upon some particular tenet; still less the church of local exclusiveness, provincial pride, or formal orthodoxy. The Christianity that is living and growing, the missionary Christianity which shall yet overcome the evil of the world with its good, is real Christianity; it is the Gospel of the Son of God in the hearts and the characters of men and women, preached through the conduct of life; and the Church of the future will be the church in any town or neighborhood which shall show to the world the most of this real work of the Spirit of Christ among men. And if we have any doubts as to just what this real Gospel is, there is one sure way in which we can learn it. Take the New Testament, and learn of what spirit, and what manner of man, Jesus Christ was. Only remember that to do this is no light thing. It means reading the Gospel of Jesus Christ with a willing mind. Have we will enough to take some single word of Jesus, and carry it with us in our hearts as a commandment through the livelong day? Are we willing to seek what the Lord means, not in the dim religious light of our churchly habits, but out in the glare of our business? Real Christianity means for us something very different, and much harder than coming to church, singing hymns or discussing doctrines. Real Christianity is not owning a pew in a church, and renting a building to the devil. Real Christianity is not contributing a farthing to missions, keeping a carriage, and paying fifty cents on a dollar. Real Christianity is not saying, "Lord, Lord," and leaving the mass of suffering humanity to take care of itself. Real Christianity is not building the sepulchres of the prophets, and guarding as sacred trusts the dead bones of the past, and being as fools and blind, when the Lord is passing by in the Spirit of an age, and calling the Church to greater works of faith, and larger visions of redemption. Real

Christianity is not professing to love the brethren, and indulging in suspicions and all uncharitableness. Real Christianity is not sitting in Moses' seat, and binding upon men heavy burdens, and grievous to be borne. Real Christianity is not—but we know too well these spurious, beggarly and hateful things which Christianity is not. What it is, something most human and divine, we see and own whenever a disciple shows Christ in some transfiguration of character to us. It is Christ—Christ loved, chosen, obeyed, as Master and Lord. It means for you and me, not only following Jesus in grateful memory along his way of mercy through Galilee and Judea, but following him in glad service up and down these streets.

There are some men among us who believe so far as they think they can, but who do not profess to believe so many things about Christ as church-members usually do. We think that, for your full salvation, for your moral growth, poise of character, and your refuge from the mystery of trouble and death which surrounds us all, it would be far better if you could believe more of the truth which we have found in Christ than you have yet seen your way clear to confess. But we would not forget, we would have you remember, that Jesus, even while teaching men of God, fixed his eye upon the heart. While finishing his work of atonement, by which all may be saved, he asked of men the right heart before God.

We wish, indeed, that all kind and reverent men, with whom, in many ways, we work in the same Christian work of overcoming the evil of the world, and making this life purer and richer, might come with us, and in humble and most reasonable confession of the divine facts of the Gospel, sit down together with us at the table of the Lord of all.

But as ministers of the one perfectly honest Man of history, whose words are spirit and life, we have always a Gospel to preach to the hearts of men which is simple as it is real. The King shall say, "Ye did it unto me," or "Ye did it not unto me." The Christ has said, "If a man love me, he will keep my word;" and, "Herein is my Father glorified, that ye bear much fruit; and so shall ye be my disciples." Surely he wants of you and me a real repentance, and a real faith, and such knowledge of God's doctrine as may come to the servant who does the will of God.

Are we willing, then, to receive Christ as we find him in these Gospels, and to let him be the Master of our business, the Friend of our happiness, the Lord of our homes, the Shepherd of our thoughts, the Light of our hearts?

III.

STANDING IN THE TRUTH.

"He was a murderer from the beginning, and stood not in the truth, because there is no truth in him."—JOHN viii. 44.

I TOOK occasion last Sunday to speak of the thorough honesty of the mind that was in Jesus toward the life of the world. I sought to describe a striking characteristic of the Gospel, which may be called its moral realism. I shall endeavor again and again to put before you this characteristic of the Gospel, and to bring our beliefs and habits to the light of this real theology of the one honest Man of history, who told the truth which he heard from the Father. For surely no theology, old or new, is worth preaching to men, if it be not a real theology, seeking always to discover the real thing in religious experience, and in the history of divine revelation. And the desire for more simple and honest reality in living and in thinking is one of the clearest notes of the Spirit in present Christianity. Along this line of a more real Christian living and thinking further progress is to be made in the knowledge of God, and in the spread of the Gospel through the world.

The chapter from which our text comes this morning shows Jesus' wonderful power of bringing men out of their fictions of life, and leaving them as though judged by God himself. The Lord's words with the chief representatives of religion in Jerusalem revealed the moral core and substance of things. Our text illustrates Jesus' habit of discovering the essential thing in life. It touches just that vital point which in our exhortations concerning standing in the truth, and defending the faith, we are apt not to see or to care for. His word was, "He stood not in the truth, because there is no truth in him." The text discloses the condition under which it is possible for a created being to stand in the truth. It shows how a stand in the truth is to be taken. It is no little thing, no easy task of a moment, to stand in the truth. It were a great and happy thing for a finite mind to stand confident and serene, like a son of God, in the truth. You may have stood some rare evening upon a mountain-top. The veil of mists had been lifted from the valleys; the highways, the villages, the rivers' course were etched upon the map of earth that lay beneath you; on the far horizon the sea and sky met in one lustrous line; the few lingering clouds showed to your eye, as you stood on that height, their upper edges turned to gold, while the whole air, under the great dome of heaven, seemed to have become one clear crystal to let the light shine through. So is it to stand in the truth. It were worth the effort of a life-time, if, after all toil and climbing, we could stand bright-souled and exultant in the truth. So without life-long toil and climbing, every hour, Jesus stood in the truth.

You perceive thus that much more should be meant than is often suggested to us by the common exhortations, "Stand fast in the truth," "Stand firm, holding the faith once delivered to the saints." Men may only mean by that, stand with us, or as our fathers stood. Be obstinate on our side. Or they may be thinking simply of standing steadfastly in some limited conception of truth, and not of standing Christlike in some large, luminous sense of God. Or we may urge one another to stand in the truth, as though all that is required of us were to stand where we are, and in what we have been taught, without once inquiring how a finite mind is to find its place sure, serene, sunny, in the truth. And particularly when men are debating about great themes, or contending against what seem to them grievous errors, the call to stand in the truth may sound like a fierce battle-call, and in bitter controversy for some truth men may even lose their personal abiding in all truth.

In this one short text Jesus puts before us the real thing to be desired in our anxiety to stand in the truth. And like all other real things of worth to us, this object to be desired pertains to a man's character. The truth must be *in* us, or we cannot abide in the truth. Jesus' word was, " He stood not in the truth, because there is no truth in him." Having no truthfulness within, the Evil One lost his standing in the truth of God's universe without him. He had fallen from the truth because there was no truthfulness within him.

This extremest case of Satanic falling from the truth illustrates the whole process of descent of soul from the truth. According to this word of Jesus, we may take it as general law, that a mortal being must himself be truthful in order to maintain his standing in the truth of things. A man cannot know the truth of nature if he cherishes a lie in his heart. The soul must itself be truthful to see the truth. When we exhort men, therefore, to stand fast in the faith, we need, if we would follow Christ's example, to look to it first and last that we and they are in our spirits of the truth. If not, we shall not find, by all our logic, sure, sunny standing-place in the truth.

I wish further to illustrate and to enforce what seems to be the simple and universal law of knowing the truth according to this deeply suggestive word of the Lord Jesus. We will begin with some of the more obvious examples of it.

First, this universe is a moral universe, and a man to stand in it must himself be morally sound. An immoral man can have no permanent standing-ground in a moral universe. I say the universe is moral, and I mean there is no untruthfulness, or dishonesty, or hypocrisy, or favor of vice, or shelter for falsehood of any kind, in the constitution and nature of things. Nature invariably gives the same answer, under the same circumstances, to chemist or physicist. The laws of things know no crookedness. The creation was made in truth, and continues in truth. The ocean-tides keep true time and measure; the sun is steadfast in its course; the atoms of matter are always the same definite regularities, and the stars are honest. Nature throughout is one piece of honest work. This veracity of nature lies at the foundation of our industries. Every railroad is built upon it; every revolving wheel of our factories is centered upon this infrustrable truth of things;

every man going forth to his labor under the sun works in faith that the earth and sky will keep their primal covenant, and all earthly happiness is nature's plighted troth kept to all living creatures, and the heart of man.

Now, then, when a man who is born to stand in a truthful universe takes up some lie into his soul, what happens? What must happen but that fate which befell the Father of lies? He cannot stand in the truth because the truth is not in him. Suppose a man conceives a fraudulent thought, and says, I will go about my business, and succeed with that fraud in my mind. What is the end? Defaulters behind prison bars might answer. They did not stand in the truth because they first turned false to themselves. It may have been a little falsehood at the start. Defalcations always begin in a man himself before, and sometimes months and years before, they begin in the office or the bank. The real beginning was not even when the first temptation to use others' money wrongfully may have presented itself. It was before that; the fall began far back of that in the man himself, when he let some falsehood come into his life; when he seemed to be more than he was; when he sought to keep up an appearance which was not true; when he let any untruth, whatever it may have been, take possession of his desire of life. And at last men were shocked to discover that he stood not in the truth because the truth was not in him.

Perhaps, however, the end has not come yet, and men who are not truthful within seem still to stand as though the universe were in their favor, and nature's honesty not set against them. It is no new thing to see the wicked prosper.

Nevertheless, the universe is a moral universe, and its forces are honest forces. Soon or late, in this world or another, the end of inward untruthfulness is certain as the law of gravitation. The moral universe can be relied upon eventually to throw out every immoral man. *Without* are the idolaters, and every one that loveth and maketh a lie. It would be necessary for moral infidels to do something more than to shut up the pulpits, close the Bible, and laugh at heaven and hell, in order to prevent the final judgment of a universe which was created in truth, and which keeps the truth to every man born into it. And we do not have to look on to the last day to discover how this law is working. Men, on account of their falsehoods in themselves, are being cast out by the truth of things. You can see it every day in business. The laws of wealth are more than laws of economics. They are laws also of success in a moral world which throws out dishonesty. A man cannot stand long in the world's credit, if the truth of personal integrity is not in him. You can watch the same moral judgment going on in society. A rich or popular man cannot stand always in good society if his heart is becoming rotten. He may be allowed to stand there too long, but in the end society must cast him out. And even in politics the moral constitution of the world is sure ultimately to prove itself stronger than the passions of men. Many a popular leader has not stood in the truth of the people's final judgment because the truth was not in him. The most fatal thing for any ambitious young man is to let his soul hold companionship with any lie.

This same condition of standing in the truth pertains, also, to work in the realm of science, where we might suppose that purely intellectual perception of truth would have no dependence upon morals. Yet nature wants character in her pupil even when teaching her laws of numbers. Clerk Maxwell's character was a part of his fitness for his high scientific work. So intimate is the connection between inward truthfulness and the power to perceive the truth of things, that personal honesty becomes essential part of preparation and fitness for the finest and best scientific work. And certainly this same law which Jesus taught has been confirmed over and over again in the history of literature. What a poet for the coming years Byron might have been, had there been in him higher and holier truth! Nature will own and echo long no poet's song whose soul is not true to her divine order, and whose heart is not pure as her skies.

Secondly, the universe is a divine universe, and no man can stand in its truth who wishes to say in his heart, "There is no God." There is a diviner presence in this visible creation than is seen. There is some divine reality behind all these shifting appearances of things. There is some secret of divinity hidden in nature's heart. There is an expression of divine intelligence playing over the face of nature. God is nearer us than we know in this infinite mystery of life and death. And what is seen and touched is not the half of the glory of this kingdom of God. Faith is standing in this diviner glory of things. So the truths of the unseen world were real as the hill-tops of Galilee to the man of Nazareth. God, the Father, was near as the human heart to the Son of man.

We, all of us, would like to stand with more vivid sense, and with calmer pulses, in this divine truth which we must believe is the all-encompassing and final truth of the creation. But we cannot do this if the truth is not in us. St. John wrote—and the same moral realism which pervaded Jesus' teaching pervades the disciple's words: " If a man say, I love God, and hateth his brother, he is a liar: for he that loveth not his brother whom he hath seen, cannot love God whom he hath not seen." Very plain, and homelike theology is that doctrine which the beloved disciple learned from the loving Master, and common people can understand it. A man is not standing in the truth of God if he is bearing a grudge in his heart, or if he is seeking to pull himself up by putting another man down, to grow rich by making every one with whom he does business poorer. We cannot stand clear-eyed, confident, and illumined souls in the truth of God, if we are false in thought, word, or desire, toward any man, woman, or child on God's earth. When a person is thinking a hateful thought he does not believe then in God. There is no God in his heart at that moment. Though he should be making an argument to prove that there is a God, no man with an undivine thought in his heart could believe in God. He is living in that thought or passion in a Godless universe. He is an atheist in his own soul, denying the very essence and glory of God, though he be saying, " Lord ! Lord !"

And it is of no avail for any man of us to try to believe in God or immortality, or the whole unseen universe, simply by thinking about them, or discussing the natural probabilities for these beliefs, unless we are first willing and eager to have some truth of God in ourselves, living and pulsating in the heart of our life, and so by the truth within us finding that we stand in the divine truth of the world. If any man of you, on the contrary, becomes so absorbed in your affairs and ambitions that you can think of your business, and little else, all the seven days of the week, and even your wife, and the children God has given you, become in your self-absorption as unreal and almost as unknown to you as angels are, and you choose purposely to live in that rush of worldliness, from lust of gain, and not from absolute compulsion for the sake of others, then you cannot expect to have any real assurance of your Father in Heaven, or of your own immortality, for the truth of home is not in your own soul. Always the truth must be in us before we can stand in it,—the truth of love, of fatherhood, of humanity, the truth of home, and friendship, and high purposes worthy of immortality, before we can stand in the truth of God, and the heavenly home, and the life eternal. Live like a brute, and believe like a son of God? No, never! We cannot do that, for the universe is truthful as well as divine, and there must be truth within answering to the truth of God without, and every falsehood in the heart is a blind spot, and every sin in the soul is a dead nerve, to the light and the love in which Jesus lived on this earth every day as though he were in heaven. Does any man among you want us to prove the existence of God to him? We will not take with us our books of divinity; we will go and search your book of life, and see if we can find any evidence of God there. And if we should find that yesterday or to-day you put down your own desires, and went and did some truth of God; if you, strong man, in your haste, stopped a moment to make that little child happy, or were not ashamed to espouse the cause of that poor man who came to you for righteous help, or if you resisted manfully the devil when he offered to give to you, or your corporation, some kingdom of this world for your compliance with his last fraud, or if you strove even at cost to yourself to see some just thing done on this earth, or in genuine repentance you sought to undo some wrong which you have learned your sin has done, then by these signs and evidences of truth in your book of life, we will bid you find God and worship him; for justice and charity, and fair dealing, and all virtue are essentially divine, and by these things within our hearts we may know the good God above us and all around us, whom having not seen we love.

And then, if we have aught of divine truth in us, we may turn to the evidences of God in the world and begin to appreciate them; we may reason of the Creator to some purpose from the regularities, like manufactured articles, of the atoms, or from the manifest providence of our human history, or from the ideas which are the sacred trusts of the soul of man.

Finally, this universe is a Christian universe, and if a man has not the Spirit of Christ he cannot stand in the full, final Christianity of the universe. The Scriptures plainly teach that all things were made by Christ, and that in him all things consist. He is the Head of the creation. The incarnation—the personal descent of the Creator, and His union with His moral creation—is not for this little world only, nor for the brief period of our history, but for the whole creation and all the ages. The universe is Christian in the sense that it was created for Christ, and reaches its consummation in the Word made flesh. It is Christian in the sense that God has shown Himself to be Christian in His eternal thought and purpose toward the world. And it is Christian because its last, great day shall be the Christian judgment. We must all appear, not before the throne of Law, or to be judged by the light of nature only, but we must all appear before the judgment-seat of Christ. The universe is Christian, and all souls in it are to receive Christian judgment.

Hence, if we would stand in this full and final truth of the universe, we must have some Christian truth in us which shall answer to the final, revealed and perfect Christian character of the universe around us. If we should fail of this, if we should fail of becoming Christian at heart, how could we hope to stand at last in the Christian universe? Whatever is not Christian must eventually be cast out as a dead and worthless thing. For Christ must reign until all enemies be put beneath his feet. Sin must go, and death must go, and all uncharitableness must go, and all deceit. For the Christian nature and character of the universe is to be revealed. "And I saw a new heaven and a new earth:

for the first heaven and the first earth are passed away; and the sea is no more." "And I heard a great voice out of the throne saying, Behold, the tabernacle of God is with men, and he shall dwell with them, and they shall be his peoples, and God himself shall be with them, and be their God." "Then cometh the end, when he shall deliver up the kingdom to God, even the Father." And God shall be all in all.

IV

THE POSITIVENESS OF JESUS.

"Verily, verily, I say unto you."—JOHN i. 51.

THIS expression is one of the signs and evidences of the divine originality of Jesus Christ. In the brief reports which are given in the Gospels of the words of Jesus this phrase, "Verily I say unto you," has been recorded by the evangelists more than seventy times. It evidently was a characteristic and habitual expression of Jesus, which, in the disciples' memory of him, distinctly marked his conversation, and separated him from all other men.

When we wish to explain any natural phenomenon, we proceed to classify it. We say it belongs to such an order of events; it is an instance of a general class of phenomena. But this "Verily, verily, I say unto you" of Jesus Christ refuses to be classified. It is an expression which stands by itself. The positiveness of Jesus cannot easily be coördinated with any other known kinds of human positiveness. It was unique.

There were in Jerusalem examples enough among the scribes and Pharisees of one kind of religious positiveness with which we are not unacquainted. The dogmatists we have always with us. The scribes, whether in theology or science, will open their books and say, "It is written," and that is the end of all controversy. The bigot will hold fast the letter of his creed, and cry aloud, "So we believe, and, without doubt, any one who does not believe as we do is beyond the pale of the true Church." Ignorance will stand firm upon tradition, and swear to all passers-by, I know. In Jerusalem, and in all times and cities, there has lived the man who could not be mistaken. This spurious kind of positiveness is not unfamiliar nor unnatural. But we cannot read the Gospels without discerning at a glance, that the assurance of Jesus Christ was wholly contrary to the blind positiveness of the learned scribes and the dogged Pharisees. The common people, when they heard Jesus affirm, "Verily I say unto you," instantly recognized the fact that he spake not as the scribes. It was not the voice of the dogmatist which the people heard in the Sermon on the Mount. It is not an immense and superhuman, but deceived self-confidence which has confronted every generation since with the Verily, verily, of the doctrine of Jesus Christ.

Neither was the positiveness of the Son of man like the positiveness of the prophets of old. We cannot possibly classify Jesus among the prophets of Israel. The nature of his assurance of God was different from the former prophetic confidence in the word of God. The prophet of old entered the city, passed through the people, and stood before the king with a "Thus saith the Lord" burning in his soul and leaping like flame from his lips. He did not say, out of some indwelling consciousness of Jehovah, "Verily I say unto you." "The word of the Lord came to me," "The burden of the valley of vision," —such was the prophet's manner of speech; Jesus alone said calmly, constantly, as one speaking directly out of his daily consciousness of divine life, and as though his word were enough, "Verily, verily, I say unto you." By this one characteristic the Son of man is separated from all the Hebrew prophets. Jesus never had been taught those words of immediate authority in any school of the prophets. Where did he learn them? Whence came to him this habitual expression of his personal, spiritual supremacy?

The positiveness of the Son of man was not in any manner like the confidence of the philosopher in his reasonings, or of the student of nature in the verification of his results. Jesus' *Verilies* precede rather than conclude his teachings. He gave no demonstrations; he collated no facts; he wrought no experiments; he carried his disciples through no prolonged processes of reasoning. Jesus Christ simply stood in the midst of men and said: "Verily, verily, I say unto you." If he worked miracles, it was not as a man would make experiments to verify for himself the truth; Jesus condescended to give disciples signs of his glory, but for himself he could say, "I know the Father."

Neither can Jesus' positiveness be classified with those rare religious faiths which his disciples may have attained in his name. For not only was Jesus' positiveness greater than the positiveness of any other man who has ever lived, but it has its distinctive quality, and, moreover, its birth and growth in his life cannot be traced, as we can follow the history of faith in the lives of his disciples.

Faith is for us an achievement of life—often the

last, as it is the noblest, achievement of a man's spirit. And we know how hard it has often been for us to believe. Our best faiths bear the marks of suffering upon them. We have been compelled to believe in order to live. There came a time when we said, Now I must believe, or I cannot live. There were moments when we might have perished had we looked down, and not up. We know, some of us, in what dear graves we have buried our doubts. We know out of what trials, and sorrows, and disappointments faith has been born of God in our hearts. Our faith is often the peace after the storm, the light that has quietly and surely dawned after hours of darkness, and long watching for the morning. And the Christ has come to us, and bidden us believe. But no Christ came to Jesus. He was the Christ to himself. There was none like him before him, no Master and Lord in whose discipleship he could see God revealed. He could go to no other for the words of eternal life. He was the first-born among many brethren. Jesus' faith was therefore original, and not derived—the witness of God which he had in himself, for there was no other who could be in God's place as the Christ to Christ. Hence, in this respect, also, the positiveness of Jesus was wholly unlike the faith of disciples in him which most nearly resembles his positiveness. He was the first of men to say of all unseen and divine things, "I know—Verily I say unto you."

In this positiveness of Jesus there is to be discerned no trace of our conflict, or doubt, our weariness of soul, contradictions of spirit and body, and hard won victory perhaps of the angels of light over the demons of denial in us. Jesus seemed to believe spontaneously and directly out of his own consciousness of God. Other children becoming men grow into man's inheritance of ignorance and spiritual uncertainty; the child Jesus grew as naturally into a divine Sonship and its assurance of God. This peculiar spiritual positiveness of Jesus marked his teaching from the beginning. It was in the answer which he gave the mother who found him teaching in the temple. We may know that narrative of the evangelist to be true to the reality, because no Hebrew disciple could ever have imagined or invented a scene so unheard and undreamed of as the picture which Luke has drawn of the child teaching in the Temple. Jesus puts his "Verily I say unto you" before his exposition of the law of Moses. And every verse of the Sermon on the Mount is firm teaching. Each blessing is clear, sure truth of God. The Sermon on the Mount with its beatitudes shines by its own light, piercing the world's moral darkness, and positive as a constellation. And never, in all Jesus' conversation, was there to be detected a hesitating note. The doctrine of Jesus throughout was sure of itself. The Gospel of Jesus is so much clear, sunny certainty. "Verily, verily, I say unto you," was his announcement of himself to Nathanael in the beginning of John's Gospel; "Verily, verily, I say unto thee,"—so the Lord makes known his personal word to Peter at the close of John's Gospel; and in all the chapters between is heard the same voice of divine positiveness which never wavers, never trembles, never ceases to sound.

The peculiar quality of Jesus' positiveness appears

still further when we reflect upon the subjects concerning which the Son of man was absolutely sure. They are the subjects of which other men are not sure. Jesus was most positive where we can be of ourselves least positive. He said, I know, where we can only say, I trust. His *Verilies* do not precede assertions concerning natural truths which we can discover or demonstrate. Jesus gave no positive teaching concerning matters of science. He did not put his verily before some announcement of astronomic laws or physical processes. Jesus left man to learn for himself, by ages of experiment, the arts of life. Neither did he put his " Verily I say unto you," before statements concerning matters of history, which the scholars, by patient studies, may search out. He did not say, Verily, verily, concerning the authorship of any book of the Old Testament. He left all such questions to the critics. Upon many subjects for which our theologies grow most contentious, with regard to which sectaries become most confident, and over which denominations are formed, parties rallied, and churches even divided, the Christ of the Gospels seems silent. We cannot find any Verily, verily, of our Lord for such things as Sanhedrims determine, and bigots enforce. The cup of persecutions which the church has filled, and which the martyrs have emptied, so that only the bitter taste of the dregs of it is left upon our lips, was never the cup of the Christ which he would give to his disciples. Open the New Testament, and follow through the Gospels for yourselves these *Verilies* of our Lord, and observe carefully at what times Jesus stands before his disciples, or among the people, in this supreme positiveness of his knowledge. "Verily, verily, I say unto you,"—the Lord is speaking of the new heart, the childlike spirit, and the true life into which man must be born again—the eternal life which he that believeth may have even here and now. He is speaking of prayer, and of God's listening to it; of faith, and its power of greater works; of the disciple who is to be as the Master in the world, and of the giving a cup of water only in his name, and its reward. The Lord is speaking, when he says Verily, of the freedom of the son in the Father's house, and of the bondage of sin, the poor slave of which cannot abide in the house forever; he is speaking of the possible forgiveness of all sins, save only the sin against the Holy Ghost—the soul's last, fatal rejection of God. When Jesus used this word of supreme personal authority, he was speaking of himself, of his power from the Father, of his place in our human history as the door and the way for all men into the heavenly fold; of his consciousness of indwelling divinity, in which he could declare, "Before Abraham was, I am." The Lord with his Verily, verily, in the midst of his disciples, is speaking of his death, which must needs be for the life of the world, as the grain of wheat cannot bear fruit except it fall into the earth, and die. And once more, in that hushed upper chamber, where he had broken the bread and blessed the cup, solemn and low, and tender as with an infinite sorrow, yet clear and sure, and triumphal as though some eternal joy were sounding beneath all its sorrow, that divine voice is heard, saying, " Verily

I say unto you, I will drink no more of the fruit of the vine, until that day that I drink it new in the kingdom of God."

Remembering these *Verilies* of our Lord, I would have you take notice, first, that over against all our human ignorance, sinfulness, and need, the Gospel is one grand affirmation of God. The doctrine of Jesus Christ is an assertion of those spiritual truths and those eternal realities of which we most need to be made sure. Oh, dear friends, if we take any of these questions of our lives which trouble us, and baffle us, and break our hearts, to Jesus Christ himself, we can find for just these vital needs of our souls, some "Verily, verily" of our Lord. There are, indeed, silences in the Gospel, and great shadows left clinging close to its luminous truths; revelation, like the starry sky, has vast vacancies unillumined between its points of lights. To our human curiosity, seeking to make God's pure will a visible, tangible thing on earth, instead of a living truth in the heart, no sign shall be given. But the Lord Christ dwells among men with some word of eternal life for all our vital human needs. Christ is present every day with his "Verily I say unto you," before your life and mine.

I have seen strange providences during these past few years meeting the lives of some of you, for which I can find in all the books, and from all my teachers, no reason and no answer. I have seen joy coming, and joy going from your homes. I have seen those you loved—and they were not, for God took them. I have seen trials seemingly out of all proportion to need and character sent to some, and others left with hardly a burden to try their strength. I have seen frail women compelled to bear the weight of heavy responsibilities which strong men could hardly carry. I have seen lives strangely crossed, and high hopes crushed to earth, and joy, after its first prophetic song in some heart, silenced, seemingly forever; and I have seen also doors of life suddenly opening of themselves, where the world had seemed closed as fate against youth's utmost effort; and, again, in some life which the storm had laid waste, I have looked and seen some flower of paradise bloom afresh, as from some seed dropped—God's spirit, which bloweth where it listeth, only knows from whence and how; and I have learned, too, little by little, what conflicts and trials, and defeats and losses, lie beneath the peace, and richness, and fruitfulness, of some dear and honored lives. The prosperity, the adversity, the change, the darkness, the storm, the peace, the sunset—all this comedy, and tragedy, and epic of human life in a single parish, and among the friends we love,—who of us can understand it, or make one music of it all? Yet still, had we but open hearts to see, there stands One in the midst of us who knows the Father, who is come to us from God. Lord, tell us of these things, of these times and seasons of our lives, of that strange event, of that hard providence, of that untimely death, of all this fret, and worry, and weariness of our life; of this seemingly lawless mingling of good and evil, this strange, forest-like blending of the shadows and the light in the life of man. Oh! Master, settle by one commanding word of thine the last question about which we disciples were disputing by the way;

The Positiveness of Jesus.

divide for us our inheritance in thy truth, make all plain to our reasons, and level to our feet, and let us go in quietness, and be content! But as we thus reason among ourselves, and question in our hearts, I hear coming from these Gospels no Verily, verily, of our Lord. He answers not a word when we would lift the veil from the future, or hear from heaven now some one of those many things which he has to say hereafter.

But if we want true hearts, and strength to do and dare; if we would learn the secret of brave, cheerful, patient lives, full of grace and truth; if we wish to live with all our souls for noble purpose and with great faiths, and immortal hope, then we cannot open the New Testament without finding some *Verily* of our Lord waiting to impart to us its power and its peace. His divine positiveness is there for all our human need to lean upon. His assurance of God is there, pervading all his Gospel; and in it, as in an atmosphere of light, our spirits grow strong and clear. For all high beliefs, for all generous thoughts, for all immortal aspiration, the " Verily, verily I say unto you" of our Lord sounds through this Gospel as the voice of God. And because I have seen the Lord Jesus Christ everywhere answering human life, meeting all the tides of the human soul, and letting them break, and grow still, upon the great positiveness of his Gospel, therefore, I believe that He is the sure and abiding Word of God. Because I have seen Jesus Christ in the midst of men putting his strength of God beneath their integrity, enveloping their personal consciousness with his presence of God's righteousness, surrounding "their restlessness with God's rest," and opening all their selfishness out into the largeness of his love; because I have seen Jesus Christ holding calm and strong in his assurance of the heavenly Father, and the eternal life, the wills of men that else would have grown faint, and the hearts of women that else would have ceased to beat; because I have seen Jesus Christ, and may behold him upon any day, and in any town or city throughout the world, going before his disciples, and answering still with his grand, triumphal *Verilies* the men and women who have followed him, and who look up into his revelation of God, and will do his will on earth, therefore, I believe Him to be the true Messiah, the Son of God, the Way, the Truth, and the Life.

Remembering these *Verilies* of our Lord, and with regard to what truths they were spoken, I would bid you observe, once more, that Christian unity is to be realized up on the high plane of this positiveness, and along the line of these great spiritual affirmations of Jesus Christ. Christ's prayer for the oneness of his disciples can never be fulfilled upon any lower plane. The churches must go up where Jesus stood when he said, "Verily I say unto you," if we would find the commanding truths beneath which we can all have one Light in our eyes, and one Spirit in our hearts. It is useless to seek for Christian unity any lower down. The valleys below are full of echoes, and in their depths who of us can disentangle the passing shadows from the eternal truth? We must seek to bring all our churches up to the clear and grand affirmation of the Gospel of God's redeeming love. And all conflicts, discords, and clamor of controversy in the world and the church should only serve to make us turn our faces the more steadily toward the Christ, who dwelt always in the simple and eternal truths of the Father among his disciples. We need to live more in these *Verilies* of the Christ and his Gospel of the kingdom of God. Our Christianity here in New England, for the salvation of men and the redemption of society, needs to care less for differences between disciples or churches; our New England Christianity, our American Christianity, nay, our missionary Christianity for the whole world, should be emptied of the contending voices and the harsh discords of the theologians and the churches, who cannot fill, with all their childish efforts, the trumpet of the Lord; the Christianity of the world needs to be filled, as a trumpet is filled, with One single voice as of the messenger from before the face of the Lord, calling upon men everywhere to repent of their unrighteousness, and proclaiming that the kingdom of God is come nigh.

And, finally, let us not go away thinking of others, but of ourselves; for there is some Verily, verily of the Lord for each one of us. You may have heard it often, and have struggled against it. It may have come to some man as a clear, definite word of duty, commanding him to pay that debt, to undo that wrong, to make that crooked way straight. It may have come to some one in the abundance of the things which he possesses, and he knew it was the word of the Lord saying to him, All mine was thine, all thine should be mine. It may have come, in some hour of better impulse, a greeting to your soul from the God who made it, asking of you less love of money, and more love of man. It may have come in some hour of joy or sorrow, for both are alike prophetic words of the Lord to human hearts, showing for you possibility of life, purer, richer, fuller than you had dreamed. Some Verily of the Lord your conscience may have heard many and many a time repeated, and you know what service was neglected and what duty left undone. It has come to some from their childhood, a voice not lost through their youth, and though now more easily refused, still, at times, moving them by an almost resistless impulse to stand up and say, with a man's noble humility, or a woman's true devotion, I too would be a disciple, and follow no other than Christ the Lord through the years, and the ages of ages. "Verily, verily, I say unto you." "He that hath ears to hear, let him hear."

V.

THE BEGINNINGS OF DISCIPLESHIP.

"Verily I say unto you, Except ye turn, and become as little children, ye shall in no wise enter into the kingdom of heaven."—MATT. xviii. 3.

I WISH to speak this morning concerning the beginnings of discipleship. We need, every man of us, to find out the real thing which is required of us in order that we may become Jesus' disciples in deed and in truth. We say that a man must be converted. And when we would think particularly of the work of the Holy Spirit in quickening souls, we speak of conversion as regeneration,—a man must be born again.

To repeat words, however, is not to get at things. And we have seen that it was the remarkable habit of Jesus to go straight always to the real thing in human life. In Jesus' doctrine the moral and divine reality of the universe flashed its truth directly into the souls of men. To be his disciple, therefore, can be to indulge in no fictitious state of mind. Jesus Christ surely can accept no discipleship which does not begin in something thoroughly honest; for whatever else the Son of man was, he certainly was the most real man who ever looked other men in the eye. He could remain surrounded by no fictions of life. The sun burns up the vapors, and in the true Light the deeds of men are made manifest. Everything around him had to become real and clear, when Jesus himself stood in the midst of his disciples.

Hence, if we would learn what the vital thing is which we ought to mean by that worn word conversion, we cannot do better than to observe exactly what Jesus required of men when he first met them. We may take it for granted, certainly, that Jesus desired to convert every man and woman whom he met in Judea or Galilee. What he said and did, therefore, will as certainly teach us what he thought men and women ought to do in order to begin to be his disciples. The one thing essential to becoming a disciple we may trust Jesus to have had upon his mind in every instance of his conversation with men.

Let us study, then, what Jesus sought in the first contacts of his Spirit with men and women.

I remark, in the first place, that he required very different things of different people. Need I do more than to remind you of the instances mentioned in the Gospels to substantiate this statement? You will remember that Jesus met Matthew, and told him to give up the publican's business, and follow him. But, on the other hand, when Nathanael came to him, all that Jesus did was to recognize him, and to leave him thinking of a beautiful vision of angels ascending and descending upon the Son of man. Once a certain lawyer stood up and questioned him, and Jesus gave to that man his first lesson in the Christian religion by teaching him, in the parable of the good Samaritan, who his neighbor was. On the other hand, a Master in Israel sought him, and in speaking to Nicodemus, Jesus said not one word about human neighborliness, but taught him how God loved the world, and how man must be born anew in order to see the kingdom of God. Again, one out of the

The Beginnings of Discipleship. 53

multitude brought to Jesus some dispute about an inheritance, and Jesus sought to put that man in the way of discipleship by giving him a plain warning against covetousness. Once a ruler of the Pharisees, who had a good house and knew how to entertain, made a feast for him, and Jesus went, as he was always willing to go among the rich or the poor, whenever he was invited; and when Jesus would convert that man to himself, he began not with one of the higher truths of the kingdom of heaven, but with a practical lesson concerning the most Christian way of giving and accepting a dinner or supper. You can read it in the fourteenth chapter of Luke. There were other people, like the centurion, and the blind man whose eyes Jesus opened, of whom the Lord at his first meeting with them seems to have asked nothing but simple and entire personal trust in himself. He did not bid them go and do anything whatever, but only wait, nothing doubting, to see what the Lord would do for them.

Then there was a man who had been possessed with a legion of unclean spirits, which Jesus cast out; and when he came down to the boat into which Jesus was stepping, and wanted to go with him and be his disciple, Jesus sent that man home to his house and his friends, and bade him tell them how great things the Lord had done for him, and how he had mercy on him. Jesus did not let that man become a disciple by becoming an apostle, giving up his business, and setting himself apart in some special apostleship; he taught him that the place for him to be a follower of the Son of man was in his house, about his business, among his friends. Yet there was a certain ruler of whom Jesus made just the opposite demand. He had been an excellent man, good from his youth up. He represented a great deal of religious respectability, and you know how hard it often is to convert that to any real sacrifice or enthusiastic devotion. That correct man wanted to know what good thing he should do in order that he might have eternal life. Many men want to *have* eternal life, as they might have a piece of land, or a property. And the Lord also wanted that man to have eternal life, but Jesus wanted him to have it really and essentially, as he himself in his daily doing the Father's will had eternal life; and you remember the very hard commandment which seemed to the apostles to be almost impossible, but which Jesus required of that man in order that he might be perfect: "Go, sell that thou hast, and give to the poor, and thou shalt have treasure in heaven; and come, follow me."

Two other instances only let me mention. Once some Pharisees saw Jesus eating with publicans and sinners. We sometimes wonder why the Pharisee takes up so much room in the New Testament to the exclusion of better things in which we should be more interested. We read the Gospels, and every now and then we come across the hateful Pharisee, and behold Jesus judging him. But the room which the Pharisee takes in the New Testament does not seem disproportionate, when we consider how much space the character of the Pharisee has taken in the history of the church. We may presume that the Lord desired above all things, if it were possible, the conversion of the Pharisees. He could pray upon his cross for his enemies. And what then did Jesus say to reach, if possible, those Pharisees? He said—and when he knew that the souls of Pharisees in all the coming years might depend upon his saying the right thing which the Pharisee must be made to hear, or he is lost forever,—Jesus said simply this: "But go ye and learn what this meaneth, I desire mercy, and not sacrifice: for I came not to call the righteous, but sinners." The theology of Jesus for Pharisees is practical ethics. The Pharisee must begin with Jesus' doctrine of common morals, if he would become a disciple of the Lord.

The other instance is the story of the Canaanitish woman. It was a disagreeable incident. Her coming seemed to have been too much even for the disciples to bear. It probably affected them as it might a Christian congregation in a city, should some haggard outcast, conscious of her need, come trembling to church, and be put by some usher in the midst of them. The Canaanitish woman nowadays, with all the devils that vex her daughters, can find her place in some Sunday meeting of the anarchists. Peter, and James, and even Matthew the publican, were respectable people. They said, "Send her away; for she crieth after us." And even the gentler John may have looked as if he felt as the other disciples did, though perhaps he was too kind to say so—and Jesus himself at first answered her not a word. There is a silence of God sometimes in the miseries of poor people, and the mercy of that silence we do not at first understand. And when Jesus at length did speak, he put before that woman a doubt and a difficulty. Doubts and difficulties are often the

Lord's ways of increasing faith. Jesus began by giving that woman a suggestion of scepticism, and its trial. I will not repeat the whole pathetic story. It is in the fifteenth chapter of Matthew. Those disciples, under Jesus' training, had become honest enough not to forget to record the Lord's words which rebuked themselves. After awhile, after Jesus had tried that woman's faith and proved it real, he said, "Be it done unto thee even as thou wilt."

Such was the way, very different from his manner at other times, in which the Lord led one poor soul to trust him forever.

Have I not reminded you already of instances enough to prove the assertion with which we began, that Jesus required very different things of different people in his first contacts with them, in order to put them in the way of discipleship?

I remark, in the second place, that Jesus required the same morally real thing of every man and woman whom he met. For, study these examples, turn them over and over, and discover the intent of the Lord in each instance, and you will see how in these different ways, and by these various methods, he sought in each case to do thorough work in the character; how he put characters to their supreme test; how his words brought each man to the dividing of the ways of his life, so that he must decide whether he would go God's way, or do something else. You can observe at your leisure the remarkable moral fitness of Jesus' tests of men to their dispositions. Master in Israel, scribe, Pharisee, publican, Israelite in whom there was no guile, covetous man, the women who sought him,—one and all, hear that word of God which is "living, and active, and sharper than any two-edged sword, and piercing even to the dividing of soul and spirit, of both joints and marrow, and quick to discern the thoughts and intents of the heart." And all those persons were instantly directed by Jesus to some course of thought or conduct which, if they had followed it, would have led them to be morally genuine and true men, even as he was true in his oneness with the Father.

I remark then, in the third place, that the beginning of Christian discipleship must be for each one of us in some real moral determination of character. It cannot possibly be anything less than that; for was not Jesus of Nazareth the true man who wanted real friends for his disciples? Our text shows this. The disciples, you remember, had come to the Lord with a question which Jesus himself never could have asked of God. It is impossible for us to conceive the Son of man asking the Father in heaven, Who shall be greatest? Those men whom Jesus had called to be his friends needed to be converted from the character which made it morally possible for them to ask such a question as that. And he took a little child, who could not have entertained such a thought in its heart, and put the child in the midst of them, and said, You must be like that child; except you are converted you cannot enter the kingdom of heaven. And then the disciples could not have mistaken the morally real thing which Jesus meant by their conversion. The men who followed Jesus of Nazareth could not remain religious dreamers. He was sure in some such way as that to awaken them from their comfortable fictions of piety, and to show them that his discipleship meant letting his divine character master them. And surely, to begin to be a disciple cannot mean anything less now that Jesus has ascended, and the Holy Ghost is here.

The Lord Jesus Christ inspired character and conduct among his disciples. The Holy Spirit is now the power of character and conduct among men. Salvation is the creation from sinful humanity of a society of true characters, and righteous conduct, for the ages of ages.

To be born again of the Holy Spirit may mean for us to have in the course of our religious experience a great many suggested thoughts, awakened feelings, inspiring desires, and even at times glad surprises of light, or rare, restful calm of heart. We cannot measure, we cannot define, what God's Spirit may work in us and for us. But to begin to be a disciple is for us to accept the truth, whatever it is, which God's Spirit in our hearts brings personally home to us, to hear the word, however simple, which the Lord is speaking to us, and to turn from whatever else we are following, and to make it our first business to do that truth of the Lord in our lives. We may find that word of the Spirit, waiting for us to obey it, in the next duty which may be sent to us from God, or it may be already in our hearts in the better thought of life and happiness which comes unsought to us. Let us be sure, however, that the real Christ from the real God asks of us real Christian determination. What the true Man who came from God to tell us the truth will be sure to require of us, is not that easy compliance with which we would confess him while we follow our own desire

The Beginnings of Discipleship. 59

of life, nor that fashionable semblance in which we think it becoming that religion should dress up social respectability. The Lord asks of those who would turn, and be his disciples in deed and in truth, that right thing which it may cost a man something to do; that generous and genuine service which you may not be ready to offer the Master; or that decisive conquest and subjection, so long postponed, of the false, worldly self, which has been keeping down the true and nobler self. Whatever may be the particular determination, sacrifice, or act of obedience and faith which lies at the beginning of discipleship for any of us, we may be positive that it is something pertaining to the heart and substance of character, upon which Jesus has his divine eye of hope, when he bids us repent and believe, and, with his disciples, come and follow him.

It has sometimes been said, or feared, by very excellent people that in the effort of the modern pulpit to teach men to live according to Christianity, as an ancient Church father put the new theology of his day, we may be in danger of dropping out or minimizing the doctrines of the Church. On the contrary, the real spiritual forces at which the Church in her doctrines has always been grasping, we would seek to bring to bear more directly, broadly, and morally upon human life and society. We would free them from any encumbrances which may prevent their laying hold directly of character and conduct. In particular, this Scriptural doctrine of conversion and the new birth needs to be preached not only as a truth of dogmatic theology, or as a formula for religious experience, but as a veritable truth of the Lord to be done on earth, even as Jesus, when he would make disciples, began by casting out devils, rebuking covetousness, exposing whatever was immoral and Satanic in men's conduct, and turning men from such dispositions and desires as were wrong, and all contrary to God, and setting them on their way of new obedience into the kingdom of heaven. Conversion! Do not let us belittle and desecrate the Lord's word by speaking it as though it could mean anything else than the most honest, decisive act and posture which a human being can possibly take in the sight of God.

To be a disciple! To become a Christian! It certainly does not mean to become perfect at one leap. It does not mean at once, and as by magic, to be a saint. But it means no little thing. It requires real moral determination. It is a religious decision. It means for the school-boy or girl to learn the next lesson as though the God who made the mind had set the task, and to try to do everything as a child of God, whom Jesus would bless. It means for the young man or woman to do the next thing which youth may find it in its way to do, out of the purest motive and from the holiest love in which by God's grace a soul may go free and glad, yet dutifully, upon its life's course, as upon an errand to which it is sent from the Father. It means for the mature man or woman to give up the false habit and to forsake the sin which may have wound itself around the life, and at any cost to do the right thing in God's sight. It means courageous repentance, and the most manly affirmation of the living soul and its conscience, and sense of immortal destiny, of which in the power of the Holy Ghost we can become capable.

And remember that Jesus Christ in his word put the two things together: You must turn, and you may enter the kingdom of heaven. Turning, and entering a kingdom,—these two things belong to Jesus' teaching concerning conversion. It is not a mere inward turning therefore; it is a change which puts the whole man into right relation and harmony with the whole moral universe, and the eternal being of the Godhead.

It is turning from the unreal, empty, sinful world, from all its wilderness, and darkness, and terror, and entering a kingdom which lies without us, and around us, and beyond this earth, full of light and companionship, which is just as real as a city with its streets, and gates, and happy homes. The disciple has his citizenship in heaven. Joining the church symbolizes and expresses this. To have the Spirit of Christ, and to be among the children of heaven, is the real thing to be prayed for, and lived for, and, when the time comes, to die for.

VI.

SIGNS OF THE TIMES.

"Ye hypocrites, ye know how to interpret the face of the earth and the heaven; but how is it that ye know not how to interpret this time? And why even of yourselves judge ye not what is right?"—LUKE xii. 56–57.

You notice that this word of our Lord was addressed to the multitude. The people were to interpret the signs of the times. Public opinion should be filled with intelligence, and judge what is right. You will observe, also, that in this instance the Lord applied to the people a word which ordinarily he reserved for their false teachers and leaders— " Ye hypocrites." The word hypocrite charges falsehood upon the character of a man. And a false character necessarily results in a false judgment of events. If the people failed of true discernment of that Messianic time, it was owing to some falsehood in their life. Make the life of the people true, and public opinion can be trusted to judge that which is right in every time. The instinct of true life is the best interpreter of God's times.

We should fail to follow the command implied in this saying of our Lord, did we not, as a Christian Church and a Christian ministry, seek to interpret the times, and on all questions to make public opinion right.

No Christian pulpit, in loyalty to this word of Christ, can hold itself altogether aloof from the providential problems of the hour. No Christian church can sit in peaceful and pious seclusion from the questions which press upon the life of the people, and remain a true witness to the Son of man. Hence, upon this first Sabbath of the new year I deem it particularly appropriate to pass somewhat beyond the range of those ordinary topics of the pulpit which concern us more personally as individuals, or as a local church, and to seek with you to interpret some of the signs of this time. Let me remind you, before we proceed to this task, that it is our mission to be interpreters, rather than makers, of the problems and the duties of the times. It has been said with profound historical insight that providence makes the problems which present themselves from time to time before the church.

I shall confine my inquiry this morning to only two of the significant providential signs of this time. I shall speak of present providential indications in the social and theological problems which are before us. The two are more closely related than may be thought. For a socialism which would push man along without any religion is laying down but one single rail for human progress. So a religious belief which does not run parallel with some practical line of conduct would be of little use to the people. The problem of history is to take humanity out of Babylon and its iniquities, and to transport it to that Jerusalem which is free. Christianity, which is the way of human progress, is both truth and practice, both theology and life. He is no friend of man who would separate the two. Our first inquiry, accordingly, concerns the social signs of the times.

We sometimes speak of the labor question as the social question of our time. But it is not. It is only one end of the social question. The question between capital and labor is not the real question before us as citizens and as Christian men, any more than the real question before Solomon was, which mother should have which half of the child. The child was one living whole, and the real question was, Who should have charge of it, and bring it up?

Society is one living, organic whole, and it cannot be split into opposing halves without shedding its life-blood. The real social question is, Who shall have modern society—the true or the false mother? Whose child is it, the whole of it? Does it belong to the devil, or to God? This has been the social question of all times, and it is preëminently the social question of this time. The church will say, the life of society shall not be destroyed by any war of classes; humanity is one body, and it must be kept as one divine creation, and in it we all must be members one of another. Any power that would divide humanity is false to man.

I point to it as one of the signs of the past year that this truth of the organic unity, the living solidarity, the common humanity of men, has been coming more powerfully into the consciousness of the people. An hour of anarchy in Chicago has aroused the conscience of the country to this truth of our social integrity. The evil and failure of combinations and strikes of one class against another class, is teaching the people anew that we must prosper together. And the social fever and excitement which sometimes seem to make the whole head of our society sick and the whole heart faint—what is not that compelling us all to see? Are we not learning that there is danger for the whole body if we let any member suffer? Society cannot drag its feet in the mire, and hope to keep its eye always clear. Society cannot continue to let its hands be unprotected or unclean, and keep its heart merry, or its brains free from attacks of delirium. If from all these labor troubles, and all this social agitation, we are learning this truth of the solidarity of humanity, this truth, as in our Christian language we would put it, that God hath made us members one of another, we shall read a sign of this time which we must understand, if the blood of the people is not to become hot with the sense of wrong, and the whole constitution of our society is not to be torn and rent by convulsive efforts for industrial liberty.

I know that some men of insight and intelligence are beginning to say the present state of the country is ominous, as were the signs of discontent and uneasiness in that period which preceded the outbreak of the anti-slavery conflict. It cannot, indeed, be denied that great masses of our countrymen are feeling a sense of grievance which they find it difficult to define. And the past year has left as a sign of what may be coming, not, indeed, the strikes which have spent their force, not the method of boycotting which has already become too dull a weapon for use, but a new labor movement in politics; and that is a sign of possible demands for we know not what upon the organic law of the land. We must recognize this sign if we would interpret this time. But over all the turmoil of the cataract, and the wildness of the agitation, I see God's sign of hope. For this also is plain, that an instinct of justice and a love of humanity are still the deepest things, and the truest, in the heart of the people. And the best mind of this country is giving itself with scientific thoroughness, yet with consecrated enthusiasm, to the study of these problems, and fitting itself for leadership of the people through these dangers. I speak now not merely of the discussion of these questions in almost every religious assembly and in many pulpits—for much of our effort may have its only use in calling more general attention to social and industrial problems which others, more specially trained, must work out in the halls of legislation, and in the business of the world,—but I refer in attestation of my statement, and as a reason of hope, to the fact that the young men who gather at the centres of education in this land are being trained in our universities to understand and to meet these social and political questions, as in my college days no young man anywhere could be trained. Our New England colleges, true to the memories of the men who founded them for country and for God, are educating our youth, the sons of rich men and of poor men together, to be teachers and leaders of the people along the lines of true progress; and the influence of men so trained will be felt in the legislation and the life of this country after the demagogue shall have fallen with his blind followers into the ditch, and the people will pass on under wiser guidance to a civilization more prosperous, more equal, and more just. It is no insignificant indication of this quiet, but potential work which is being done at our universities, when rich men in Boston begin to inquire what influence at Harvard has led their sons to develop an unusual interest in the condition and ideas of laborers in their employ; and it is a gratifying sign also of this time of social agitation and hope, that a graduate course of training in these subjects marks the new era of the old Yale. "The scholar," to quote a phrase which I heard during my college days and have not forgotten, "receives the people's oil, and is to return it to them in light." The Christian pulpit, too, wherever, at least, it has felt a fresh breath from the Spirit, is inspired with the Lord's word of the Gospel of the kingdom, and is preaching the truth not merely of individual election, but of the redemption of the world in Christ, and the election of all believers to service and to usefulness for the kingdom of God's sake.

I pass now from the mention of this most interesting sign, and succession of signs, of our time to the consideration of the signs which are apparent in the theological sky.

A glance through the past is necessary for any appreciation of recent theological signs. In the New Testament is to be found an Epistle to the Romans. The very title marked a new era in the history of the true religion. Christ was preached to the Romans. And one distinguishing characteristic of the style, and of the whole mode of approach to the truth of Christ, in that Epistle is its adaptation to the Roman habit of mind. St. Paul was fitted and chosen for that special work. St. Paul was himself a Hebrew lawyer. He had been trained in a school of Jewish law; and besides that, he was a

Roman citizen, and as a Roman citizen probably understood something of Roman law. With that Epistle to the Romans there begins the Roman conception of Christianity. It is a forensic presentation of Divine truth, such a presentation as Roman lawyers might appropriate. Its practical principles concerning the duties of the strong to the weak are particularly fitted to Roman character and Roman Christianity. This conception of truth which the Apostle, who could be all things to all men, so wisely presented, and which he was chosen and inspired to begin to teach, has been wrought out through a long history of controversy and creed. A distinguished jurist has lately had occasion to point out how thoroughly the Roman jurisprudence has saturated our traditional theology. "The principles of the Roman law colored theology after the Reformation as well as before." Some time since a friend narrated to me the difficulties in the way of a profession of faith, which a thoughtful person had experienced who had been brought up under current notions of Christianity. Those difficulties were not doubts of the Gospel of God's love in Jesus Christ our Lord. They were found to resolve themselves mostly into difficulties with the Roman law conception of Christianity, as that conception has been elaborated in certain received formulas, and imposed as a test of sound belief. They were difficulties which might more properly be charged to the code of Justinian than to the Gospel of the Son of man.

Some of the ordinary phrases which are familiar to us in our Protestant creeds have been transferred almost bodily from the Roman law. Now, observe,

I beg of you, that I do not suggest that this conception of Christianity, and its development in our Latin creeds, is altogether false, or was unnecessary. It is, in its way, and rightly understood, a true and helpful conception. It may still be useful to us, for example, to conceive of Christ's atonement under the old common law principle of the payment of a debt by an accepted substitute, although that legal form has fallen into disuse, and few are familiar with it. I do not deny that the truth of Christ could adapt itself without untruthfulness to the Roman habit of mind, because that would be to refuse to accept as canonical the Epistle to the Romans; neither do I deny that this whole Latin and legal conception and systemization of Christian doctrine, although it has been carried far beyond the scope of the Apostle Paul's argument to the Romans, has been a most necessary and providential development, and that it has borne important fruits which remain for our use and profit. But my point is that this whole Roman era of Christianity is evidently in this century coming to its period.

I state this as a fact which is too evident to be denied by any one who is familiar with the history of modern theology. Now I want to make plain to you, if possible, in a few words, the significance of this fact as a providential sign for us to interpret. I may make what I would state clearer to legal minds, perhaps, by comparing recent change and, as I believe, progress in Christian theology, to the advance which has been made in modern jurisprudence. The parallel is more illuminative because our jurisprudence and our formal notions of Christian doctrine have, as was just stated, much that is common in the phraseology of the Roman law. The progress of modern jurisprudence, as I understand it, has been made mainly in what Jeremy Bentham distinguished as the adjective portion in contrast with the substantive portion of the law. There has been to some extent a re-codification of law, but the progress has been mainly in modes of procedure. The change has been mainly not in the substantive, but in the adjective, not in the essential principles of law so much as in their mode of application. And in the simplification of modes of law, in methods of bringing principles of law to bear more directly and really upon cases, progress has been made, and much progress remains to be made. Now, precisely this is what the theology which began in this country with Jonathan Edwards, and whose end of improvement is not yet, has been doing, and will do. The essential principles of the Gospel have not been abandoned, and they will not be. They are older than any of its existing forms. There has been no loss from the substance of the Gospel, but there has been much gain in the simplicity of the adjectives. We have not abandoned, indeed, all Roman forms of presenting the Gospel, but we have declared that we will not be bound by them. And I am sure the mode of procedure has been simplified, and will be still more in all our churches. We have been reviving the older Greek theology, and have dared to think with Origen, and Clement of Alexandria, and with Justin Martyr, and with St. John, as well as with Calvin, and Augustine, and Irenæus, or in contact with that one side of St. Paul's many-sidedness

Signs of the Times. 71

which is presented particularly in the Epistle to the Romans. And the one common motto of the theology of this present time is to be found in that old saying of an ancient father, " Let us learn to live according to Christianity." Such, it has been justly observed, is the distinguishing feature and sign of a living and hopeful theology, " Let us learn to think according to Christ Jesus."

I have spoken of this movement, which is now quite general and powerful, as a movement which began with Jonathan Edwards. He accepted, for he had no other choice, the theological and philosophical forms of his day ; but his spiritual being overflowed them, and his spiritual thought to-day is flowing on in broader channels than he knew. The theology of New England has always carried in it a spirit and a life which could not be confined in the swaddling clothes in which its infancy was wrapped. It broke loose from Calvinism by grasping boldly the principle of a universal atonement for all men. It shook off a Roman limitation in its abandonment of the idea of mankind as being bound, like one Roman family, under the headship of Adam—the federal theology as it used to be called, and which was regarded by many in its day as the faith once delivered to the saints. It proclaimed with no uncertain sound the individual responsibility of every sinner before God. It still subscribed, but in no servile subjection, to the Westminster Standards—the Catechisms and the Confession of Faith—which were statements of doctrine largely legal and political in their origin and their forms. But it went boldly back to the New Testament, and sought to become a disciple of Jesus himself. It dared believe that the non-elect nations are not enemies, and it became a missionary faith. It would be disloyalty to the best traditions of our New England theology, and bondage to a yoke to which our fathers would have given place by subjection, no, not for an hour, should we not follow still onwards the way of God's providence through the new problems, and among the new sciences, and in the light of the growing revelation which God is constantly making of himself in the history of his redeeming love. I hail it then as a happy sign of our times that we are working out anew our forms and our statements of belief to answer the vital necessities of faith, and to meet the demands of the world upon a Christianity which is to be light for the Oriental mind in India as well as for ourselves. And I hail it as a hopeful sign of the times that the instinct of the religious public, even with swifter and surer discernment than the minds of many of us clergymen, who have been trained in the theology of the Latin confessions, has discerned this need of a simple Gospel for the missionary opportunity of the present.

I will suffer myself to allude but briefly to the controversies of the day through all the alarms and the clangor of which the new missionary era of Christianity is to be rung in. These controversies and agitations are peculiar to no denomination, and they are originated by no men. God sets the tasks of his church in every age. Our problems of faith and life are providential problems, and all churches, nay, all parties even in the churches, under God's overruling wisdom, are working together for the greater good and the further advance of Christ's kingdom.

In our own denomination, the general movement which I have been describing has been obstructed temporarily, or held back, at two separate points, and two controversies have arisen. Of one of these* I will not suffer myself at this time to speak. Of the other, I will remark that the difficulty which has arisen, and which is still unsettled, in the administration of the American Board, may involve some temporary loss of money and of men to missionary service, but it should involve on our part no loss of steadfast loyalty toward the work of the Board itself. Policies change, and men change, but the cause of missions is the cause of Christ. And it is my firm belief that, as the final result of this whole painful controversy, all obstructions will be removed which may now lie in the way of the best educated and most catholic missionary service, and that whatever traditional opinions or objections in the administration of the Board are now preventing our churches from sending as missionaries our young men who are prepared to teach in the spirit of free and reverent Christian scholarship, as they have been taught in our best theological seminaries, are obstacles and obstructions to the kingdom of God which are destined erelong to be swept away before the rising public opinion of the Congregational churches, whose servant, and not whose master, the American Board is.

Two signs of the times are meeting, and their interpretation is not obscure,—on the one hand an

* The Andover Controversy.

open door for the Gospel to the higher classes of the pagan world, and on the other hand the education of young men, in our leading theological seminaries, to meet with broad and comprehensive Christian wisdom the thoughts of men in all lands. If we are wise to discern these manifest signs, and will bravely follow the indications of God's will in them, we shall see this century close in grander missionary triumph than our fathers could have dreamed. And the dawn of another of the days of the Son of man is already in our skies. Let our faces be toward its blessed light.

I would turn with hopeful earnestness now to the younger members of this church and congregation. I would have you feel that you are living in one of the days of the Son of man. I would show you that this is a Christian world, and that you may find Christ's work everywhere to be done in it. I would have you see what is coming to me with ever stronger conviction, that in Christ, and in the company of his disciples, you can find life worth living, and your characters can become complete and radiant. The new year has begun. The old is gone. The past of this church is secure; its future is with the young men and the young women to whom I preach. Give to all its work your help and your enthusiasm. And if we should be permitted to stand together at the close of this greatest of the Christian centuries, and some who are now consecrating their early youth to the Lord should be found still looking on into years of service beyond any possibility of my age then, may grace be given me to bid you still go forward. bound to the past by no teaching of mine, with minds free to follow whatever truth of God may still break from his Word, or be made manifest in his constant revelation of himself in his works and in redemption, with no fetters upon your thoughts, but with the cross of Christ upon your hearts. And on this first Sabbath of another of the years of the Son of man, I would ask again some who are not numbered with us, but whose hearts are already Christian, to be truer to themselves, and to become more helpful to others, by taking upon themselves with us the vows of the Lord's house.

VII.

THE NOTE OF UNIVERSALITY.

"𝔒𝔯 𝔡𝔢𝔰𝔭𝔦𝔰𝔢 𝔶𝔢 𝔱𝔥𝔢 𝔊𝔥𝔲𝔯𝔠𝔥 𝔬𝔣 𝔊𝔬𝔡?"—1 COR. xi. 22.

IT is important for us to put the work of the local church in its right Christian setting. The single congregation is a unit in the great multiple of communions which constitute the Church of God. The Church of the living God is the large, redeemed humanity of which Christ is the Head, and of which all Christian communions are the members.

It is necessary for us that the kingdom of God should be localized for our service and devotion in single and separate churches. The strong emotions of men's souls gather around definite objects. We want something near, distinct, realizable, to which to give our utmost efforts. Men in battle look to their regimental colors for their rallying-point. The country is localized to their eyes in those colors, and brave men will cling to them under hottest fire. Yet those colors would be nothing of themselves, did they not belong to the country and represent the country. Thus the devotions of Christians gather in our local churches and in our separate denominations; yet these would not be worth the service of men, did they not all stand for the large idea and represent the grand truth of a redeemed humanity, the Church of the living God. To follow the colors of a particular church or sect for its own sake might prove to be treason to the Church of God. "For the Kingdom of God's sake" is the motto which should fly upon the flag of every church in the world.

I wish this morning, accordingly, as a fitting preparation for our annual church-meeting, to direct your thoughts to this sign of universality which belongs to the true Church, and which must be kept, therefore, upon its banner by any individual church which is to represent in its place the Church of God.

The Church of God is a universal institution for man. The Church is for humanity. The Church belongs to all men, although all men may not consent to belong to the Church.

If we listen to the Gospel which Jesus came preaching, we cannot fail to hear ringing in it this clear note of universality. It was the Gospel of the kingdom which he came preaching. It was not a Gospel of individual election merely, nor of personal salvation simply, but the Gospel of the Kingdom which he came preaching—the Gospel of a redeemed society organized in righteousness, and vital with the Spirit of love—the Gospel of the kingdom of Heaven.

The daily life of the Son of man was marked by this sign of universality. Jesus' conduct never could be contained in the measures of the scribes and Pharisees. His life overflowed Judaic limitations. It was every day the life of man for man. As such it was a constant surprise to his disciples. The one thing that perplexed the scribes and baffled the chief priests was this universality of Jesus' sympathy and teaching. It was a larger humanity than Jerusalem could understand. The publican wondered at his kindly word, and the common people never heard man speak like this man. On almost every page of the Gospel some incident brings out, or some passing word of Jesus reveals, this universal humanity of the Christ. All the barriers which national pride, religious customs, or Pharisaic misinterpretations of God's words had built and made impassable between man and man, Jesus ignores in his conduct, or sweeps away with his resistless grace. Recall, for example, that scene at which the scribes and Pharisees were shocked, when Jesus sat at meat with publicans and sinners. Recall that scene at Jacob's well at which even the good disciples were surprised. Not even the ancient law of the Sabbath, hedged about as it had been by the strict interpretations of the Rabbies, could restrain his divine humanity. He healed the impotent man, and restored the sight of the blind on the Sabbath-day, and proclaimed that even an institution so sacred to God from the completion of the creation as the Sabbath was made for man.

This note of some universal good for man to man, to which Jesus' daily conduct was keyed, pervades also and harmonizes all his doctrines. No teacher like the Son of man had ever used the universal adjectives in speaking to men. He did not use the language of election and discrimination. His call was for the many. Come unto me, all ye that labor—if any man have ears to hear—if any man will come after me—whosoever, therefore, shall confess me—whosoever shall do the will of God. We cannot take these universals out of the speech of Jesus without taking all the music from it.

Jesus' words of life are for humanity. His divine speech of redemption is for man as man. Jesus' promises are for us as individuals because they are for us as men. Because we belong to the world for which God gave his Son we can hope to have part in its final redemption. Because we bear the common human nature which he took upon himself, and in which he made confession for our sin, and was obedient unto death, we can have personal part in that forgiven, regenerated, and restored humanity in Christ in which God shall be glorified.

I have just been reminding you how universal were the teachings and the life of Jesus in their sympathy and significance; but the Person also of Jesus is distinguished from all others by this sign of universality. For when we wish to designate Jesus of Nazareth, to describe him by the one word which is most distinctive of him, what is the name which is his as it belongs to no other? He has named himself in his human place in history, "I, the Son of man." "The Son of man goeth as it is written of him." "The Son of man must be lifted up? Who is this Son of man?" When the disciples began to realize who and what manner of man the Son of man was, the other confession followed of itself, "Thou art the Christ, the Son of the living God." And upon the man who first learned and confessed that whole truth of the Son of man and the Son of God, Christ said the church should be built. To Peter in his first clear, conscious confession of what Christ is as the Son of man and God, the Lord gave the promise of his church.

The church, therefore, whose promise was given in

that moment of the disciple's discernment of the divine human Person of the Christ, should be characterized by the same note of universality, and marked by the same sign of sympathy and significance for all men. It is not to be a chosen school of disciples around their Teacher; it is not to be a national church—another temple in Jerusalem; it is not to be a state church—a new Rome over the whole world. Not as such a Master and Lord had Peter discerned the Son of man to be, whom he confessed as the Son of God. Peter had recognized, dimly and darkly it may be, the divine humanity of the Lord Jesus Christ. There would still be needed the vision of the sheet let down from heaven, and the call which came to him from Cornelius—that righteous heathen man who was to have the Gospel preached to him for his salvation,—and there would be needed also the marvelous inspiration of the day of Pentecost to fit Peter and to make him ready to lay the foundation among the Gentiles of the church of the Son of man. In due time the needed enlargement of his knowledge of Christ was given, and afterward through all the Apostle's preaching and epistles we can hear sounding the same note of universal grace and divine love for the world which was struck in the song of the angels at the birth of Christ, and which pervades, like celestial music, the speech, and doctrine, and sacrifice of the Son of man.

I hold, therefore, this idea of a universal good for man to be the true idea of the Church of God—the idea to be derived from the Gospels and the Person of Christ, from Pentecost and from Peter, and from all

The Note of Universality.

the apostles, at least after Pentecost. It is the idea not of some select society, or exclusive body, or isolated communion of men, but the grand, inspiring idea of a society in which all men are to become one, of a body in which all particular groups and affinities of men are to be members one of another—of a Church of the living God for the world.

How, then, is such an idea ever to be realized? Is it in any manner coming to realization on this earth? Or is this also a dream — a Christian dream — of humanity? A far-off vision, unsubstantial as a dream, will not satisfy the present social, Messianic longing of our world. It would not be enough to point men who are hungry to the empty sky and say, See what golden color rims the far horizon. It is something—indeed, often it is very much—to be able to give to people a brighter sky for them to live and to toil under. Religion does give bright, pure sky for life, where otherwise there would be no outlook, and only darkness. But more than this the religion of Christ in our churches is required to do for the people, if our Christ be the true Messiah. A hungry world wants not merely colors of transfigured clouds to delight the eye and to cheer the heart; it wants heaven's light as that light has been taken up, transformed, and offered freely to it, in good wheat and corn; and the churches of God are to be the fields and granaries in which the light of the Gospel is converted and gathered up into the bread of heaven for the life of the people.

The churches are called, in the name of the Son of man, to represent and to begin to realize on earth this true society, this large, generous, redeemed humanity, which is the Church of the living God. And although the actual Christianity of an age may seem to lie in sharp contrast against this divine ideal, even as a low fen may lie in dark contrast beneath a sunset, nevertheless, let us keep this ideal shining in our eyes, let us cherish in our hearts the inspiration of this hope of a Church of humanity. And perhaps never more clearly or hopefully has the way been shown in which the city of God is coming from heaven, than it is revealed by the course of Christianity in these latter days. For this is preëminently the age of missionary Christianity and the missionary church; and what is that but the beginning of the holy catholic Church universal?

Three days of the Son of man, at least, in Christian history have preceded our day. The first was the Apostolic age, that day of glorious beginnings of Christianity. It was necessarily, however, an era of but partial applications of Christ's words to the life of the people. The Apostolic Church must struggle for its right to be in the Roman world; it could not reach out and lay hold in every direction of Roman manners and institutions. The Apostles were called to liberate and set in motion the Christian ideas, but not to apply them universally to their world and its customs. The time, for instance, was not yet come for Christianity to meet, and to settle, according to Christ, the question of human slavery. Paul indeed planted the Christian principle of liberty in the epistle to Philemon. Put all the sentiments of liberty together which may be extracted from the Greek and Roman classics, and they would not yield the principles and power of human liberty, sure in time to grow and to come to their hour in history, which were potential in the Church-life that Paul planted and Apollos watered.

After this age of Apostolic beginnings and partial applications of the Gospel to society there followed in God's educational providence the age of the power of external law, and the era of the outward unity of the Church. The Roman age of Christian history witnessed an external universality of the Church. The Roman idea of unity and universality as a distinctive note of the Church of God was profoundly true; but its method of realizing that idea on earth was the way of Cæsar rather than the way of the Son of man. A return from Roman Catholic supremacy to the authority of the Son of man followed next, in the divine order of history, through the reformation. And now that through Protestantism and Puritanism we have been brought safely back from the Latin Church to the Apostolic Church— what is the next step forward as the signs of the times show the way in which the Son of man may be discerned still going before his people?

Obviously the providential tasks which are laid upon our present Christianity, are compelling the churches to take some further step forward; or they will die out if they stand motionless and idle in the old ways. Look about you, observe the devouring wants of our industrial civilization, and judge for yourselves, if this necessity of further progress be not a question of the life of our present forms of organized Christianity.

For what are the chief questions of life now the world over? Clearly, they are social problems.

And what are these social questions? Disputes between those who work, and those who win? between those who have little, and those who have enough, and to spare? No, no. These are only the surface agitations of life. The social question goes deeper. It is a broader and profounder problem than any passing strife of labor and capital. How shall men learn to live together? Common physical necessities force this simple, yet hardest social question upon modern society. Because men burn coal, for example, they must come to some understanding as to how men are to live and work together. How not only in this city, or this country, but how in the whole world shall men live together? That is the real social question, and all labor troubles, or wasteful competitions, or hurtful combinations, are symptoms and signs of this social moral question, this vital problem of society. And it is a world-question. No country now by any tariff or embargo can take itself out of the world. No nation can live for itself alone. The fates of the modern nations are bound together. The problem of healthful and prosperous civilization in one land is involved in the problem of healthful and prosperous civilization over the whole world. There is nothing so foreign that it may not become domestic to any country. The destiny of this world, it is increasingly evident, is to be one destiny.

To the Church of God providence is bringing home this one social question of the world. How then are the churches to answer it? Not in the way of Rome. The imperial age is past and gone. The Son of man will not be enthroned as Cæsar. There is no way of legislation to the millennium. The kingdom of heaven is not coming through modern legislatures. Once the Roman Church brought the people under the law, and it was good for the world that it was brought into some order and unity. The Latin genius for ruling was providentially used in the development of Christ's kingdom, and the strong Roman mind of Calvin also was called of God to rule Protestantism for a season; when however the necessity and the age for that talent and that service are past, then a survival or forced imitation of it may become obstructive and hurtful.

How is the present Church to meet this present social problem of the world? In the sixteenth century the old man of Rome, swollen with corruptions, was not sent to do God's work, but the Lord called the new man of Protestantism to sound to the nations its bugle note of Christian liberty. Neither shall the old man of Protestantism, shrunken in muscle, its separate members scarce hanging together, bound helplessly to its past, mumbling its creeds of better times, and living on the income of its capital laid up in more fortunate days, be the new man of the coming day, fearless of the light, strong in hope, going forth unbound and unburdened, in the unity of the Spirit, and with Christ's constraining love in its heart, to cast out the devils of our modern civilization, to heal the sufferings of whole classes of men, and to preach, The Kingdom of heaven is at hand.

Verily, the days are coming—are they not now at hand?—when the Son of man will open his mouth, and bless the multitudes in our churches, and in the power of his Spirit our Christianity shall become as never before the Church of God for the world. We are to see more of this redeemed, and true, and satisfied humanity here upon this earth. The churches are becoming more deeply conscious that they exist not for themselves, nor for the salvation of their own members only, but for some divine blessing for all men. The true Church is a divine institution which belongs, like the creation itself, to mankind, and in which all men born into this world have divine rights. The Church of God is an order of human society, a hearth of humanity, a household of God in which, according to God's eternal purpose in Christ Jesus, every human being has birthright and promise of redemption; and it is the mission and the work of the churches to proclaim to every creature that the Church of God belongs to them, and that as men for whom, every one of them, Christ tasted death, they have gracious rights in the Church of the living God. The Church belongs to you, whether you will belong to it or not. The Church is for the world, whether the world now be for or against the Church.

I have been speaking of a large subject—too great for a brief sermon. But I shall reach my aim, whatever else be left unsaid, if by these remarks I may succeed in putting our thought of our local Church, its history, its present work, its future promise, into this larger thought of the Church of God, holy, catholic, universal, which is for mankind, and which shall be the final society of this earth. I am sure that if we can gain and keep, even in our hopes and dreams, this larger, divine idea of a world-church— a church for the world,—belonging by a divine order

The Note of Universality.

to the world, and not permitted to stop or rest in its social and missionary endeavor until it becomes in fact, as it is in idea and power, the Church of the world,—we shall, thereby, receive an inspiration and a joy in our particular church-membership and our special church duties which we can find in no other way.

Two further consequences of great moment follow from this truth that the Church, by the decree of God's love for the world, belongs to mankind, and that the Church in the end is to prove itself to be the world-church, the pure and happy society in which heaven and earth are reconciled.

The first of these is that we who belong to particular communions of believers should be careful in our administration of them not to interfere with the divine rights of any man in the Church of God. "Repent: for the kingdom of heaven is at hand," Jesus began to preach. Our authorized missionary message still is, Repent and believe, for the Church is here as the sign and witness of that kingdom of God. We must look carefully to it lest by incidental beliefs, or temporary forms, or rules of expediency, we preach some other Gospel, and exclude some souls from our churchly participation in the kingdom of God. All men who come as disciples of Christ, have divine rights to any table of communion which is spread in the name of Christ. If Christ be indeed set forth here, there is no heathen man or publican who has not the right of one of the children of God, and one of the Lord's brethren, to be present and to commune where Jesus himself is present in the midst of his disciples.

The missionary motive of the churches lies also in this Gospel of the kingdom, and the claims of the world upon disciples of the Son of man. All men have gracious rights in the name of Christ to some communication of the Gospel of a universal atonement. The divine rights of the world to the Church, and in the Church, impose upon us the present and urgent missionary obligation; and all beyond our power to accomplish belongs to the gracious responsibility for the world which God in Christ freely assumed upon the Cross. The commandment which the ascending Lord gave his apostles is consonant with his life and death, and with the essential character of his Gospel, which is to be preached to every creature. Such is its nature and intent; it is its essential character that it is to be preached to every creature,—to the utmost limit of present possibility by us, and beyond our power, how, or when, or where, we may not know; for no man of us has revelation or authority to determine the times and the seasons of the coming of the Son of man to men.

The other consequence of this truth is the following: men who are already in the Church have right to stay there, and to work out honestly and patiently within the Church any questions or doubts which may trouble them. A Christian man in the Church has the right of a disciple to meet with a candid mind all facts which may be discovered, and to study all questions which may arise before his reason. The disciples of old were constantly going back to the Son of man with some new question, or from some fresh perplexity. We have the rights of students, the rights of honest minds, the rights of reason, to life-long inquiries within the Church of God. The worst faithlessness is to dodge truths, and to be afraid of facts. Still, the Son of man as of old, dwells among the questionings of men. I speak explicitly and with emphasis, because I know there are men already in the Church who sometimes wonder whether amid all their mental difficulties, and with the questionings of their growth in knowledge, they have moral right still to belong to any church. Nay, the Church of God belongs to you, and you have a birthright in it. Your hearts having been there almost from your childhood, your desires of life being there to-day, you have within the Church of God a man's right of reverent thought before the Lord. Until you have made up your mind to take all that you have, and go to a far country, you have the right of a son to your Father's house. And there is no better place than within the communion of the Church for you to meet the questions of your lives. Many difficulties and doubts you can settle better in the company of disciples than you possibly can in any other fellowship. And nothing pertaining to the life of a true, growing, honest soul should ever be deemed foreign to the communion of the Son of man. Every truth of the creation that ever shall show itself to be true, belongs to the Church of God. And surely in the most consecrated society of souls the final truth of our human life and death can best be studied and known. So Thomas of old kept in the Church, although he doubted. He knew that the best place where he might learn whether the Lord was risen indeed, was the place where the disciples were met together. And though he was a doubter, and had not hid his doubt, the disciples did not think of closing against him the door of the room where their Lord might find them and him. And so, Thomas, the honest sceptic, became an honest apostle. For every Thomas who has accepted the word of the Lord, "Repent: for the kingdom of heaven is at hand," although he may not yet have learned to say with an undoubting mind, "My Lord, and my God," the Church, like the disciples of old, can surely afford to keep some place within its chamber of communion, until Thomas shall also see for himself, and worship.

In conclusion it follows from this truth that the Church of God belongs to mankind, that every man to whom it is presented has some corresponding obligation towards it. A divine intention for man creates a duty on the part of all to whom it is made known. We hear this note of universality in the Gospel, and to it our lives should make prompt response. This divine fact that God has on earth a Church for man, that there is to be gathered in the name of Christ a true society of men, renders any self-isolation, or unwillingness to throw ourselves into this divine order of human life, or Church for man, a serious failure on the part of those to whom this divine call comes.

The world is redeemed in Christ, and it is a sin and a shame to live in it as though it were not a redeemed world. There is a Church of God, already begun on earth and in heaven, forming, growing, expanding, having a glorious world-task committed to it; and it is ignoble not to have part in it and its work. There is to be a new heaven and a new earth, and all true and generous life which shall not have shrunk in selfishness, and shrivelled in sin, and hardened in impenitence, until like a dead bough it be fit only to be burned, shall be quickened, and perfected, shall blossom and bear fruit, in that kingdom of heaven.

VIII.

ZEBEDEE'S ABSENCE.

"Then came to him the mother of Zebedee's children with her sons, worshipping him, and desiring a certain thing of him."—MATT. xx. 20.

BUT where was Zebedee? Why did he not come too? His sons and his wife were with Jesus. How happened it that Zebedee never was found with his family among Jesus' professed disciples, and that he alone of his family was not at the cross? It has been conjectured that at the time of the crucifixion Zebedee was dead. He may have been waiting then in some other world for the full manifestation of the Redeemer's love. Or possibly Zebedee may have lived for weeks and months after his two sons had followed Jesus, and after his wife also had gone up to Jerusalem to minister to the Master, and yet for some reason he may never have found occasion, or improved his opportunity, to appear with his family among the confessed disciples of Jesus Christ.

There is only one clear notice of Zebedee in the New Testament, and that puts him before us in a not unfavorable light. When Jesus at the beginning of his public ministry was walking one day by the sea of Galilee, he called James and John, and they left their father with the hired servants in the boat, and followed him. Zebedee made no objection. He was willing they should go. We can see him in the boat, looking up at the sound of a call so strange from One who was already beginning to speak with authority, and saying not a word against it, though his sons left him to mend the broken nets, and went away over the hills with the wonderful stranger. Yet that silent acquiescence must have cost Zebedee something. His sons were full-grown, and capable of being very helpful in the boat. And Zebedee was growing old, and needed their help. Although he had hired servants, he must still go himself to the shore, and look after the boat; and the lake must have seemed lonelier to him after his two sons were gone. Many a man since has let his sons follow some noble cause, although the call took them from himself, and changed all his plan of life for them.

And Jesus who called James and John, we may be sure, could not fail to notice Zebedee's sacrifice when he let them go without a word. The Lord had not asked Zebedee also to go with them. The hard ways which he must tread with his disciples might have been too toilsome for the father of James and John. He may have been too old for that service. Jesus called to be his apostles comparatively young men. They would have erelong work to do exhaustive of muscle and nerve, as well as taxing their faith. Jesus chose robust men in their vigor for his apostles and witness-bearers to the world. But though Jesus might not call a man like Zebedee to be an apostle, he did ask of him a disciple's sacrifice; and Zebedee's still faithful, though lonelier work in the boat, with the hired servants, may have been his part of the service which Jesus desired of his disciples.

We may reasonably suppose, moreover, that Zebedee, who could let his sons leave him and follow

Jesus, and who afterward suffered Salome his wife to go up with them to Jerusalem, must have been at least in a general way interested in their religion. He could hardly have kept on an indifferent spectator of the life and the work of the Nazarene which had cost his home so much. Even if not personally and openly a disciple he must have been pleased on the whole with his sons' new faith, and glad also to have his wife religious. And he was willing still to work faithfully for his family, and to pay the bills, whatever their religion might cost him. The apostles must have somebody to provide for their living expenses. Neither can we doubt that James and John, as they had opportunity, must have been interested in informing their father concerning the marvelous works, and more marvelous words of the new prophet whom they were beginning to know as indeed the Messiah. They would not have been true sons, had they not taken every opportunity to let Zebedee know what they had found in Jesus Christ. And it may have been through their word and influence that Salome their mother came afterward to be known among the women who ministered to Jesus.

Leaving all conjecture however one side, and thinking of Zebedee as favorably as we may, the single fact which appears from the New Testament narrative is, that at no time after that first call of James and John is Zebedee seen with them among Jesus' disciples. His mother comes with the sons, worshipping him, but not the father. The family of Zebedee is never seen, all of them together, in any house where Jesus is, nor at the cross. And dropping all conjectures about the reasons of Zebedee's absence, I wish to speak further of this fact, which is too frequently repeated in the history of our churches, that often the family fails to appear before God in the church as one Christian family, and that usually it is not Salome, but Zebedee who is not there. This fact particularly in our Protestant churches challenges attention. It is not in accordance with Christianity. In one passage, it is true, Jesus taught that he came to make a division in families, to set even mother and daughter at variance; but it is evident that Jesus looked upon such separation in families as an incidental, and sometimes unavoidable result of the preaching of his word, but not as the intended and proper result of the Gospel. When Jesus took the pains to go with his disciples to Cana of Galilee, and to manifest his glory for the first time in a human home, he showed how God in his purpose of redemption meant to bless and to use the family. Jesus evidently meant to save the family in his kingdom. And Christianity would be less than Judaism, if it should fail to make the family the unit of the church. For the Old Testament brought families as families under the law of God. They went up to offer sacrifices by families. No member of a Hebrew family thought of being absent from the paschal meal, and least of all the head of the household. The old dispensation was a salvation of men by families. This Old Testament religion of the whole household may have been indeed an outward and formal kind of salvation, a legalism rather than a religion; but the point is that the salvation which was of the Jews, externally at least, was a family affair, and a social salvation. And Christianity cannot be less than Judaism. It must be more, as it becomes a real salvation of families of men, and a redemption of the whole civil state in the kingdom of God. We must not forget that the Christian Testament closes with the sight of the city of God on earth.

Jesus Christ, it is true, meets us individually, and gives us personally his commandment. His teaching still singles us out, and when in some solemn hour a soul is confronted with the divinity of Jesus Christ, it will seem to it as though it and its God were alone in the universe. Yet intensely personal as the Gospel certainly is, it is also the Gospel of the kingdom, and the Christian family is the true unit of the redeemed society. Infant baptism attests this fact, and we shall miss one whole side of revelation, from Moses to Christ, if we lose this view of the true religion as the covenant of God with the Christian family.

Since then it is not according to Christianity that families should be divided in religion, but is in accordance with Christianity that the family should be the living, organic unit of the kingdom of heaven, it follows that there must be something wrong somewhere, if our Christianity is not composed of Christian families, or, in other words, if in our application of the Gospel we bring in Salome, and leave Zebedee out. There is something contrary to Christ's intention in such a state of religion in the world. And if our religious faith and life be the true thing, the real thing, the absolutely good thing, which we believe it to be, there is no reason why any man of us should be content to let the religion of the family be monopolized by his wife and children.

Even in the pagan religions, in the old Roman home, the images of the gods were set in the common room, and not hidden away in the women's apartments. Christianity would prove itself to be a religion less powerful than some pagan superstition, if it should lose a large proportion of men from its grasp. It will not always do this, for Jesus was the Son of man, the Man of men.

When however I would go further, and locate the trouble, or the breaks, in our present transmission of the power of Christ along the complex lines of family and social life, the exact points of failure are not always easy to find.

I can imagine several reasons why Zebedee may have been absent from the place where Jesus might be found, when I think of the reasons why sometimes only the mother of Zebedee's children is to be seen now in the church, or at the prayer meeting. And the reasons are not altogether faults on one side. Indeed we can never be sure that we have found out the wrong in another until we have first looked for the wrong in ourselves. If James and John had misinterpreted Jesus to their father, or if Salome whose family pride at first seemed to be a considerable part of her religion, had given him some hard idea of what following the Master meant, Zebedee might thereby have been led to toil on by himself in the boat, when, had he only known, and gone once for himself to see Jesus Christ, he might have come back to his nets with a light in his heart that would have lighted up the whole long nights for him as he went fishing on Galilee.

We have reason enough to inquire whether we are giving to men such report of our Master and Lord as must command their consent. We know—if we have ears to hear the thoughts of men's hearts we cannot help knowing—that a great many Zebedees now-a-days are not to be found in professed discipleship because of a certain passive unbelief which has settled upon them. There is, on their part, at least, a felt inability to believe some things which are commonly held as Christian beliefs. And *over*-belief in the pulpit has had something to do in provoking unbelief just outside the church. Over-statement at least of beliefs has had a tendency to produce unbelief in many minds. And that unbelief lies like a fog-bank around our churches, not active and vehement, a storm which might blow itself away, but an atmosphere heavy with doubt, and cold. I have just intimated that a natural reaction of over-belief in men's minds is unbelief. Let me not, however, seem for a moment to forget that in Christianity there is commanding truth. There are revealed truths to be studied, and to be thought out in all their logical deductions to the utmost power of our understandings. Systematic education in divine truths is a part of the work of the church to be begun with its children, and to be continued to the end of old age. But all the truth which is to be studied by the disciples as they follow Christ, and which may be learned in ever larger and happier meanings in the course of Christian discipleship, is not to be forced

Zebedee's Absence.

upon men in a body of divinity as a condition of their discipleship. The first and main thing for men to discover and to own is whether they are willing to let the Lord Jesus Christ master their character and their conduct. There are many doctrines of the church, and corollaries of the Gospel, which they can more profitably study within his church after they have settled that main proposition of Christianity for themselves.

Yet I knew a man who was, I believe, a devout man, and who throughout his life had been a cheerful supporter of the church—and what report of Jesus Christ did the church, with which through his wife he was connected, bring to that man in order that he also might come to Jesus in its communion? It gave him a confession of faith which had been cast in the heat of the Unitarian controversy, all the parts of which had been soundly riveted together, and which then had been left for all future generations as the faith once delivered to the saints. The Apostle James would hardly have comprehended all of its technical phrases; the Apostle Peter might have found in it more things hard to be understood than he read in the epistles of Paul his beloved brother; and Paul himself with his trained Rabbinical intellect might possibly have so interpreted it as to be able to accept its reasoned dogmas, while John might have asked why in so complete a compendium of Christianity his one word "God is love," and, "Little children love one another," had been left out. But that was the witness of that church to that man of the doctrines of the Divine One who spake not as the scribes, and who went about doing good. Not one article or word of it did that Zebedee of whom I speak openly deny; only while Salome went to the Lord's table, he kept quietly on mending his nets. He too has gone now to receive, I trust, his first communion in that world where Christ promised to drink the cup anew with his disciples, and where Jesus himself may say to him in his simple divine way, as once he said of old, "Ye have done it unto me;" and, "This do in remembrance of me." My brethren, these days in which our lives are cast are times of great possibility for the true church of the real Christ. These are days in which men, a great many honest men, would rather believe than not believe. The powers that have come into competition with Christianity in the work of saving society are seen to be failing. Upon all thoughtful men the conviction is forcing itself that some thoroughly honest and commanding religion is needed to govern this world, and to prevent modern life from sinking swiftly into the hell of its own lusts and lies. The hour is most opportune for simple and sincere witness to Jesus Christ. Oh fools and blind, if we waste this hour of the Son of man in saving our truths and our pride of opinion, when a world in its sins waits to be saved in the name of our Christ! There are men, and women too, who do not believe because in their hard lot and struggle the kingdom of heaven has not been brought near enough to them by their employers for them to see how it belongs to them also, and not to the higher classes only. There are men who do not believe because they have not found our Christianity going before them in the way, and compelling them to honor it, wherever there is a wrong to be made right, a soul to be helped, a fair wage to be given, a debt to be paid, a devil to be cast out, or a home to be filled with the Holy Ghost.

There was Zebedee trying to earn an honest living by hard work. And he was willing to let James and John go, and live for something better. He was willing to let Salome go and look after them on the way to Jerusalem. But if they had come back from Jesus Christ disputing among themselves, and calling each other hard names, looking with suspicion at each other, and denouncing each other, because they could not understand alike some word of their Lord, and forgetting all about the poor Galileans, and the lame, the halt, and the blind, whom they had said Jesus had come to save,—do you suppose Zebedee would have joined their church?

While we may not always justify ourselves, we cannot, however, let any Zebedee off without having somewhat also to say to him, if he persists in keeping to his boat while his wife and children go and find Jesus. Even if we do sometimes make clumsy and cumbrous work of our testimony to Christ, Zebedee has heard enough of Jesus to know that Christ is infinitely nobler than we, and worthy of a man's whole soul. I do not care to speak now of the obviously wrong courses or the evil things which keep men away from the family religion and the church. I will only suggest that possibly Zebedee was too old a man, when Jesus brought the rest of his family into his discipleship, to feel that he could make any great change, or go so far as Jerusalem.

I want to speak, however, particularly of the way a man will sometimes be holden by a one-sided exaggeration of some good quality in him. I want to point out what seems to me the frequent one-sidedness of manhood in your unbelief. For instance, some man of us will say to himself, "I must be honest with my own thoughts, I will not be tempted to make-believe more than I believe." And you ought not. True godliness cannot begin with any intellectual jugglery. But the mental honesty upon which you rely is not the simple and easy thing which you may think. It is vastly easier to be honest with dollars or stocks in one's hand, than it is with thoughts and desires in one's heart. Real honesty of mind requires a thorough combination of many virtues and habits, and among them, and above all, it requires a genuine manly humility. Indeed I do not believe it to be possible for a man to have a proud mind and an honest mind at the same time. Our reason is too feeble a spark, and the mystery of things too infinite, for us to think and question except as little children. And Jesus' call was, "Come, be my disciple." Then again any one-sidedness of life must throw a man out of right relation or fair position towards some truth. It is quite possible for us to stand so closely under one influence, or so habitually in one relation of life, that we may become incapable of large, roundabout vision. The other evening I wanted to know if the sky were clear, and I looked up, and saw over me a black sky. I supposed the stars were hid. But I was standing under an electric light. When I walked on, and looked up again, the stars came out. There is a man who is living under the light of his one science. And it is honest, white light. But in it he loses sight of the whole heavens.

He needs to go further on in his life, and, not to quench his science, but to widen the circle of his experience until he too can see the ancient stars again. Or here is a man who is living in the light of his professional study, a lawyer, a physician. He sees some things in a good light; and he wants to see everything else in the same light. Talk to him about spiritual truths, and he wants you to prove them to a jury, or demonstrate them as you would anatomy. And very likely that man will not receive the passing prophet's word, so long as he stands still in that habit and position. He too needs to step out from under his own blinding light, in order that he may gain faith's larger vision. May be he is a young man playing at life, and fooling with all knowledge. Let him begin to live in earnest, if he wants to know in truth. Let a man be more than a man of business, more than a man of science, more than a man of professional habit of mind. Let him live in an ever widening experience of life. Let him marry, make him a home, and work to provide for it; let him meet with the needed enlargement of himself every child that God gives him. Let him not only go to his office, his laboratory, or his books, and think; but let him stop by his hearth, and look into the life of trust and love and hope, in which he lives as a man, and there let him think. Let him look love in the face, and think. Let him look death in the eye, and think. Let him in the long years look at the empty places by his side, and the remembered faces of the children whom he has lost, and think. Let him think, honestly as a man may, earnestly as a man can; but let him think as a man, and not as a lawyer; let him think as a man, and not as a scientist; let him think as a man, and not as a scribe. Let him think as a man, having within him the spirit of a man, and praying for the Spirit of God whose thought must be the ultimate truth of all things without. Let him think as a man must think when his soul rises within him in its divinity of conscience and its immortal desire; let him think too of the larger, nobler, holier self, which he might have been.

And to such thought of life into which the whole heart as well as the whole mind has grown,—such thought deep as love, true as spirit, honest as conscience,—let the Christ of these Gospels come. "Every one that is of the truth heareth my voice." Let the Christ of the Gospels come to you,—not our report of him, not the Christ of the creeds, but the Christ whom such thought of life may find in the Gospels, meeting all its conviction of truth and sense of need with the words of eternal life;—and then, if no sin breaks the vision, if no habit of indecision puts aside the task, in this thought of life and of God, and with the disciples' trembling confession upon your lips, receive in remembrance of Christ the simple emblems and assurance of the kingdom of heaven.

IX.

THE CHRISTIAN REVELATION OF LIFE.

"And then shall be revealed the lawless one, whom the Lord Jesus shall slay with the breath of his mouth, and bring to nought by the manifestation of his coming."—2 THESS. ii. 8.

IN a passage in "Modern Painters" John Ruskin reminds us of the delight which we are wont to experience in view of a bright distance over a comparatively dark horizon. At sunrise, beyond some line of purple hills, we have seen the sky become a great space of light, and through the shadows of the night which were still lingering in the valley, and clinging to the face of the rocks, we have looked into the dawn. Or at evening we have gazed out over the gloomy sea, and seen the restless ocean breaking upon the horizon in a line of troubled waves against the bright, quiet sky.

In the Bible we are always looking over a foreground in shadow into a bright distance. In the Old Testament prophecy the waste and tumult of history were seen against the far Messianic glory. However bleak and barren the earthly prospect, the sky beyond was a glory of the Lord. In the New Testament the Apostles have learned to see all wickedness of the world horizoned by the manifestation of the coming of the Lord. And in truthful Christian vision these two aspects of human life and our world-history should be viewed together. It were partial and false vision to separate the two. If we have been compelled to observe the evil of the world around us, we need to look on until we can see its darkness immediately beneath the brightness of the Lord's presence. If we must see just before us some hard way, some dark waste of life, all fissured, gloomy, and forlorn, we need to gaze steadily on, and to behold the near foreground against its background of some divine light and peace. We never have the full, large vision until we do. And on the other hand we must not shrink from any knowledge of the evil of the world. Faith must have open eyes for the worst facts of human life. If some boat were stranded amid the angry waves, and men were shouting for present help, it were idle and cowardly for us to stand gazing into the far evening peace. The good shepherd will go seek the lost sheep on the mountain-side, and not wait for the coming dawn. There is a prospect and a glory for us to contemplate beyond all the evil of the world, and there is a work also for us to do in the midst of the sins of the world.

The knowledge, then, of the sin which exists in human life, and also the heavenly prospect,—a quick sense of the present evil, and some vision of the manifestation of the presence of the Lord,—these two belong together, these must be made part and portion of one and the same Christian view of life.

Observe how Jesus always seemed to see both aspects of our life. Those woes of his Gospel are heard breaking beneath its calm blessings. The sin of the world was an ever-present fact to Jesus; but he saw it all set in the holy love of God. Because he saw the darkness against the eternal light, the restlessness beneath the heavenly peace, he could at once condemn sin and rejoice over it. This same double aspect of human history is constantly kept before us in the book of Revelation. We hear the confused shouts of the warriors; we see the dead bodies lying in the streets of the great city; we behold still another beast coming up out of the earth; but also there is a sound as of a great voice from heaven, there is that sea of glass mingled with fire, and them that come victorious from the beast, standing by the glassy sea, having harps of God; and when all the woes of history are over, in the world's far, bright background, is that vision, of which we never tire, of the light clear as crystal of the holy city coming down out of heaven from God, having the glory of God.

A similar juxtaposition of these two aspects of human life characterizes the chapter of St. Paul's epistle from which I have taken our text. It is in some respects an obscure passage. We do not know exactly of what St. Paul was thinking when he wrote this description of the man of sin, and of some hindering power. But it is clear that he saw this double aspect of life, the darker foreground, and the bright distance, the mystery of iniquity still working, and the manifestation of the coming of the Lord. And our text comes still closer to the necessary relation of these two, and discovers the law by which the manifestation of the presence of Christ follows the revelation of the man of sin. The revelation of sin is necessary for its judgment. As soon as the man of sin becomes revealed, then follows his destruction in the brightness of the manifestation of the Lord. When we see sins rapidly revealing themselves, we know that the hour of their destruction draws nigh. Things often have to grow worse in order that they may be better. Evil must come to full revelation in order that it may be consumed. Let us think of this more closely.

Such has been the law of the revelation and destruction of evil in history. We can discover this principle of the divine judgment at a glance when we survey great historic masses of sin. Consider for example the sin of Babylon and its destruction. When her abominations were full, God's judgment brought all her pomp, and the noise of her viols, down to hell. It was not over Babylon in the wanton beginnings of her iniquities, but over Babylon the great, that the mighty voice was heard proclaiming, "Babylon is fallen, Babylon the great is fallen." So was it of those two Romes, the pagan and the mediæval Rome. The Goths and Vandals were let loose from the quiver which Providence held in the right hand of its power, when the vices of a decayed civilization had filled up the cup of wrath which was held steadily, until it was full, in the other hand of God's providence. And the papal corruption was ready to be revealed, and ripe for destruction, when Luther sounded his appeal to the nobles of the Christian nation. God's day of judgment follows the revelation of the man of sin. What availed the hesitating voice of some solitary New England divine, or the words of the Spirit to John Woolman among the scattered Friends, to check the growing system of slavery in this country? Both North and South were making money by letting it alone. And our fathers laid the keels of the slave-ships, and the

The Christian Revelation of Life. 109

wages of that sin found their way back to Northern ports. But all the while slavery was growing up under the law of God's judgment. Whether the tree bear good fruit or evil, Providence does not make haste to shake the branches, or to lay the axe at the root, until the fruit be ripe. Jesus in the parable suffered the vine-dresser to give the fig-tree, that had been barren for three years, a fourth probation before he should cut it down. Providence lets the wheat and the tares grow together until the harvest. And when at last that man of sin in this country was fully revealed, the compromises which had restrained the full growth and revelation of slavery being taken away,—then came the hour of its destruction in the manifestation of the glory of the Lord.

Such is the moral law of progress in history; we behold iniquity brought to revelation, and then Christ's presence consuming it. There is always therefore reason for hope when we see some evil thing coming out of its concealments, and making its power felt with a more shameless impudence. Long ago a few prophets of humanity may have cried out against that hidden evil. And most respectable citizens said, It is nothing. But God let it grow. It begins to trouble some class of men. Its baneful shadow creeps over some whole section of civilized life. Its woes among men are brought to revelation in the newspapers. Even commercial selfishness grows vaguely aware that something is going wrong. And then very likely people rush together and say, "We must do something," and the first things they do very probably make the evil worse and worse. But all the while it is growing and waxing worse under the divine law of judgment. That evil thing, whatever it be, intemperance, the power of the saloon, or greed, or lust, or ominous monopoly, or social anarchy, if indeed it be growing worse, is but filling up its measure of iniquity in order that it may be revealed and consumed. Then when its woes have been heaped up beyond endurance, when its mystery of iniquity has worked itself out in our world of sin, it shall be revealed, and brought to nought by the manifestation of the coming of Christ among men.

This law of divine judgment under which evil grows, and is doomed, is a reason for courage and hope in all Christian work. Something may have given you a moment's revelation of the man of sin in this city. You may have seen in some instance of dishonor or shame the mystery of iniquity which is now working along these streets. And by that glance, and moment of discovery of the sin of a city, you are thrown back in discouragement, and you are tempted to say, what is the use of our charity, or our feeble Christian endeavor against such powers of evil? Or in thinking some Christian thought, or trying to carry out some idea born of love, and therefore of God, you may have run straight against some dead wall of indifference, or found some custom fortified against you, or some wrong method entrenched in some good institution. And because rebuffed where you expected sympathy, rebuked where you asked for aid, or suspected as an alien where you went as a friend, you drop the work to which God sent you; or, if you keep on, it is with a heartless persistence in your cause.

But have you failed to look up and on until you

saw some bit of God's sky at the end of your way? Have you forgotten that in proportion as you come to a knowledge of any evil thing, in that same proportion you have reason to believe that it shall be revealed in its evil, and be consumed? If it has discovered its sinfulness to us, if we are sure we have seen the wrong and harm of it, we can be equally sure that it will in its time be made manifest, that sooner or later whatever hinders its coming to revelation before the consciences and in the hearts of men, will be removed, and then it shall be consumed in the brightness of the Lord's coming. And is not this the reason why those men who really have seen evil things, and fought with all their might against the sins of the world, as a rule have been not only the bravest men, and the most self-sacrificing, the martyrs, the heroes, the reformers, but also the cheeriest, the most hopeful men? It is your indifferent man to-day, the man who does not lift a finger to take any burden off from men's shoulders, the man who has not the soul to commit himself against any wrong, who fears that the country is going to destruction, as it might for all of him. But let a brave soul once be aroused to anything which is wrong, let him see it and know it as contrary to God, and untrue to the Spirit of his Christ, and then as he realizes its sinfulness and is forced to discover its ancient power, and its entrenched might even in Christian civilization, or in the church of God,—how he will see also around it the glory of the manifestation of the coming of the Lord, and in that knowledge both of the evil and of the glory of his Lord, he will keep his faith, and his hope, and his patience, and that joy too in his work in which all good can be most divinely wrought.

The same principle obtains with reference to our individual salvation. Sins one after another come to revelation in our lives, and, as they are revealed, will be consumed in some manifestation of Christ, if indeed our hearts are Christian. They are revealed to us in their sinfulness in order that they may be destroyed. Under this principle we gain a clear view of what a man's conversion may be. He has gone on in a life which was not satisfactory to his conscience or heart. Something happens to bring that dissatisfaction with his position or his conduct to revelation. He sees that it is not true character. He sees a larger, more generous, altogether diviner self rising before his present self, rebuking it, condemning it, ready to consume it as by the presence of Christ. That is a crisis for any man or woman. And if we disown the man of sin in us, our false self, partner with all the sin of the world, and own the Christ-self, which may be our real and eternal self, companion with the angels of God, then we are converted, then we have passed from death unto life, then we are saved children of God. And every time any sin comes to revelation before conscience in our hearts, then is God's opportunity of grace for us. Some ancestral sin, some inherited evil disposition, may have been latent in us, almost unknown by us, for years and years. And then in some flare of temptation we see it, and read the mark of the beast upon it. It is judged; it is condemned already in the revelation of it; it is consumed, God be praised! in the brightness of his coming. That sin may not be a very gross sin capable of great beastliness. When it reaches its full measure, and is revealed, it may not prove to be a vehement passion, or devouring lust, but only some little meanness, some small selfishness, some slight untruthfulness, some dullness and bluntness of being to noble or generous things. Only a little sin! But the least sin of our hearts would be great as a shadow over the whole heavens, if we should think of it as imputed to the character of Jesus Christ. And at last we see it. That we know was ungenerous. That is not right. It is an evil thing, wholly contrary to God. Then let it be consumed in the presence of Christ. That revelation of its sinfulness is our time of grace. In that disclosure of it the Spirit is saying to us, "Behold, now is the accepted time; behold, now is the day of salvation." And there is one benign peculiarity about this law of the destruction of sin through its self-revelation in the Lord's presence. The purer and nobler the character grows, the sooner does the mystery of iniquity which now worketh come to revelation in it. The more a soul is flooded with God's light, the sooner is everything of this earth earthy in it marked for destruction. The sin of the world which in that criminal was revealed in an awful deed, and brought to its judgment, is the same sin of the world which that Christian child was quick to recognize in an evil passion, and whose falsehood and hatred long ere this may have been consumed by the brightness of Christ's presence in some mature and consecrated life. And the progress upwards is one of ever-increasing quickness of perception of evil, and power over sin. Life's slowest, hardest work is usually at the bottom. We climb, and toil; the saints seem lifted up, and borne by unseen hands towards the gates of heaven.

Such is the benign law of growth in grace; but its alternative cannot be escaped. If the man of sin in us is revealed, and we will not let him go, what then? The sin must be punished. That is sure. God cannot hold heaven safe in one hand, and let the sin of this world escape from the other hand. The man of sin must be destroyed. That is the inevitable consequence of the omnipotence of righteousness in the universe. And if we cling to the man of sin, how can God himself separate us from its fate? We must go where the sin goes, if our hearts cleave to the sin. We must fall where the sin falls, if we hold fast to it. You know that is so in this present world. Why should it be any different in any other world? Every man here clinging close to his sin, goes with his sin, is hurried down the predetermined course, and meets the certain fate of that sin. You see that happening with men who cling to deadly sins. A crime will come to its hour of revelation, and carry the criminal with it to its doom. All dishonesties go straight and sure towards ruin, and eventually carry the defaulters with them. The decreed course of a lust in this moral universe is marked by the signs, earthly, sensual, devilish, and the end is death. Down that course the man who clings to his lust has to go. If a sin comes from hell, and reveals itself to be infernal, and a man gives himself up to it, then to the hell reserved for that sin he must go with it.

This law that whithersoever sins go, they take *their*

men with them, is not only true of deadly sins at whose deadly consequences we shudder; but it is the law of the working of all sin. It holds true of every evil thing. If we are unkind or cross, we have to live in the atmosphere which that ill-temper creates. If we are ungenerous, we have to dwell in the cell which miserliness inhabits. If we will cherish small, churlish views of our duties to our fellow-men, we shall walk all our days between the dead walls where such dispositions find their beaten track. We can often see how men are living in some small, dismal world, because they choose the company of some petty sins, or are kennelled with ill-favored habits, when, if they would only break loose, and be the Lord's freemen, they might walk forth in large, helpful, and sunny lives. And many and many a time they may have seen their sin revealed,—all its uncouthness and meanness mirrored for a moment in some Christlike character which passed by them along its nobler life. Do we not remember that hour, it may have been years ago,—do we not know that moment, it may have been to-day,—when we saw something wrong in our mode of life, something imperfect in our thought of ourselves revealed? It came clearly out—what we are, and are doing—and just above it, a luminous revelation, what we might be, and ought to do. We are better or worse for that hour. For remember that this law of the revelation of sin unto judgment works downwards, as a law of death, in precisely the same way in which it works upwards as a law of life. On the one hand, the more prompt to give up anything false and evil a soul is, the quicker the sin of the world comes to revelation in conscience, and the less is the smoke of the torment of its destruction in the brightness of the presence of the Lord. On the other hand, the less willing a human soul is to repent, and be converted from any sin, the duller grows the power of the soul to perceive its sinfulness, and the severer becomes the necessity of its judgment. Hence, even if we be finally saved from the sin unto death, is the harm of putting off, and putting off, the things which we know we ought to do and to be. Hence the urgency of the Gospel to us now. Hence the pressing reason why some of you ought to take your position at once and with decision in that circle of light, and communion of all the saints on earth and in heaven, to which your parents brought you in your baptism. In the open and clear discipleship of Jesus Christ, where the Christ of God stands in the midst of all who are of the truth, and the glory of God is round about him,—there is the one place in all this world of sin and death for us to be found,—there our lives, so earth-stained, and so marred and broken, may be brought to perfect revelation, and the man of sin be consumed from them in the manifestation of the presence of our Lord.

X.

RECONCILIATION WITH LIFE.

"Nevertheless I must walk to-day, and to-morrow, and the day following: for it cannot be that a prophet perish out of Jerusalem."— LUKE xiii. 33.

SOONER or later we all of us have to learn to say those words, "I must;" and our whole character, good or evil, saved or lost, will depend upon the way in which we learn to say, "I must." How we should learn to say "I must," is the subject of this morning's sermon. The tone and temper in which we become able to use those words may indicate a moral difference between men great as was the separation between the desperate Jew in the time of the calamity of Jerusalem, and the Son of man when his hour was come.

"Nevertheless I must walk to-day, and to-morrow, and the day following." Not to the Son of man alone, but to every man there come inevitable days of life. No human will can escape the necessity of saying at some hour, "I must." Even Napoleon has his St. Helena. We say, "I will;" and the next day find ourselves saying, "I must." God never suffers us to say the one for many hours without compelling us to say the other. Thoughtlessly we go our way, and look up to find ourselves facing the inevitable. There it is, steadily confronting us. It is hard as the face of a precipice. We cannot go around it.

We cannot climb over it. We must stand still before it. There is no word of our English speech which we more cordially dislike than this same short word *must*. We will not brook it when spoken to us by other men. Any friendship would be broken by it. Love knows nothing of it. Liberty consists in refusing to speak it when kings proclaim it, or any foreign might commands it. Men have died rather than yield to it. Yet nature every day compels us to say it, and hard providences often wring it from broken hearts. There is a strange contradiction between our vital instinct of freedom and this inevitableness of so much of human life. We do not recognize this variance between constitution and necessity in other objects which have their appointed places in the order of nature. We are aware of no contradiction to the nature of matter when we say the molecules of oxygen and hydrogen must combine in certain definite proportions. It would be no insult to a star to declare, it must keep true time over our meridian. Nature is one ordered compulsion. But from the first impulse of infant consciousness our human nature rebels against inevitableness. The child always has to be taught the habit of obedience. There is some spiritual power in us evidently created for a free life unrestrained by outward compulsions. Sin is wild outbreak of free-will, and its curse. But the principle of rebellion against the power of nature over us, and our objection to any outward control, is a constitutional principle of human nature. It is born in us, and we can never be content to say, "I must," unless we can say in the same breath. "I will."

Yet consider how large a portion of our daily life is put before us, and how much of our own personality is given to us under some form of necessity; and how large consequently is the work of reconciliation to be accomplished, if it be possible, between the *I wills,* and the *I must,* of our lives. There is, to begin with, the *must* of heredity. We cannot vacate our inherited individuality and choose another, and a happier. We have to accept ourselves as we were born. "Which of you by taking thought can add one cubit unto his stature?" There is a *must* for every human face and form in every lookingglass. There is sometimes an awful inevitableness in the laws of heredity. "Your mother was an Hittite, and your father an Amorite." "Thus saith the Lord God unto Jerusalem: Thy birth and thy nativity is of the land of the Canaanite; the Amorite was thy father, and thy mother was an Hittite." So the prophet Ezekiel explains the false Israel and his apostasy.

Besides this primal necessity of our birth, there are the fixed grooves of natural law in which our lives must run, and all the forms of circumstance to which our individualities must be fitted. In the midst of these physical, industrial, and social necessities our space of spirit and freedom seems small as the cage of a bird, and hard sometimes as the treadmill of a beast of burden. Every day, every hour, has its limitations and thraldom of spirit for us. The dawn of day in which the careless birds sing, brings renewal of burdens to men. The round of cares must be run through again. It is for us, "You must," "you must," every step we take, every effort we make. And this little earth still holds us as in a vice. We can see the heavens, and know that there must be wondrous spectacles, scenes magnificent beyond all comparison, in those distant constellations, but we cannot follow our thoughts to the nearest planet; we have not yet the freedom of the skies. Even our arts mock us by disclosures of things which we cannot touch, or handle, or own. Photography reveals stars which cannot be seen even in the telescope. The mighty universe opens around us; but we are tethered to one world, and must be content with a dwelling-house, and a daily beat of duties, on this insignificant earth until we die.

In addition to this general and constant compulsion of the world upon our free spirits, to which we have become so used that only in thoughtful moments do we rebel against it, there are sent to us hours when it seems like death to have to say, "I must;"—that hour when our hope and all its bright colors broke like a bubble, and we knew in cold disenchantment that it must be so; that hour when the bearer of evil tidings stopped at our door, and a few hurried words subjected our hearts to the inevitable;—those hours when we must enter the vacant home, and live on in memory where we would hear a present voice, and see a vanished face. Every grave means, "You must."

And there is a law of death working in these members. There is an inevitableness of change and decay witnessed even by our pulse-beatings. And by all our immortal instincts we resent it. The law of death is something foreign to us. It is a bondage of spirit to live in the fear of death. We were not made to cease to be. Pain is an insult to the spirit. Sickness is humiliation of the soul. Death is the triumphing as of an enemy over us.

I have been expressing thus our common feeling of irreconcilableness to much that seems inevitable in human life. In order that we may learn to say "I must" in any true and free way, we should look more intently into the nature of this great compulsion which is laid upon us all. What is it? It wears ofttimes a face of fate. Is that its only and eternal countenance? Is there any thoughtfulness for us behind it? What or whose is this will which must be done on earth as in heaven? Our tone and temper when we say "I must," will depend very vitally upon our belief concerning the character of the Power whose grasp is the inevitableness of human life. To what voice, and to what voice alone, in the universe may a man answer, "I must," and "I will"? For this also is true that there can be no reconciliation for us with the inevitable, no happy harmony of our spirits with our circumstances and our necessities, until in some way we have learned to answer, "I will," from within our own free hearts, whenever that Voice from without speaks to us its inevitable, "You must." The two voices from without and from within must become one, keyed to the same note and making one music, before life can be harmony and peace.

My friends, the ways in which men have tried to harmonize these voices are familiar to us, and we know what discords have been left in human life. We know too well what indifferent success we have often had in seeking to make one music of our necessities and our desires of life. We know that every way except one of the many which have been tried has failed. We can hope to gain nothing by setting our lives to old tunes which have not worn, and which never were happy efforts, even when master-spirits tried them. Some tunes for life long ere this have been played, and played out, in human history. Stoicism was one, with its monotony of suppressed emotion. Buddhism was another with its want of vital movement, and its one repeated note of passionless resignation. Epicureanism has been another, with its light notes, suited only to life's lightest passages, and its want of voice and harmony for life's deepest motives, and its saddest, holiest hours. These, and all variations of these tunes for human life, have been played and repeated over and over again, and not one nor all prove to be accompaniment enough, true, and pure, and always fitted for the ever-changing movement, the depths and heights, the passion and the peace, of a human soul in this mortal life.

I have noticed, also, that the men and women who still try to suit life's necessities to these modes and fashions of reconciliation with it, never persist long in any single method which may for awhile seem to them sufficient. They are stoical, or light-minded, resigned or rebellious, passive slaves to life, or violent non-conformists, by fits and starts, as they meet now this, now that, inevitableness of their destinies. They have learned no secret of deep and abiding reconciliation with nature, fate, or providence. They have their moods, not their victory over life and death. Perhaps most often they succeed for

Reconciliation With Life. 123

a season in chilling and hardening themselves against life. There are human hearts like our lakes in winter-time. The winds do not ruffle the surface. The deep waters are not moved in grand waves. There is no pleasant ripple and play of feeling over them. There is thick ice above, and stillness beneath. So we may freeze ourselves into equanimity, and a heart encased with ice need not be troubled. Few men, however, can remain frozen in Stoic unconcern through all the seasons of this mortal life. And that is not life. Arctic isolation is not life. For this human hearts were not made. If the equanimity of a block of granite be the chief end of man, evolution marched towards its greatest failure when it presumed to go beyond the age of primeval rock, and began the ascent of life to end in the human brain and the human heart; for the living soul cannot lie still under all influences as a dead stone. All ways but one of being reconciled to life have failed; —how can we most clearly see, how can I help every young person find, that one way in which once a human soul like ours became reconciled to all things, in which human hearts have been joined in happy union to strong, eternal law, in which the word "must" has become to many a word of spirit and of life?

I might say that it is religion which does this blessed work; that I have seen religion reconciling men and life; and that religion has joined soul to life so happily that henceforth no man can put them asunder. I might urge that only when we gain clear perception that every inevitable thing is a divine thing, every word "You must" in our life a word of God, only then, can we begin to answer with good heart, "I will." I might set in order the reasons for believing that beneath this whole appearance of inevitableness in human life and history there is a will of divine righteousness, and a heart of infinite love. When we feel the touch of the love of God in the hand of fate, our hearts can say through all our tears, "Thy will be done." I might urge further that our present life with its civilized temptations, and its polite lies of the devil, and its fashionable demons of unbelief and unrighteousness, lays upon all true men an urgent necessity of realizing the presence of the living God on this earth, if indeed we would keep the faith and the hope of a man's spirit amid the shams, and shames, and tumults of our world.

I might urge you to try this religious way of reconciliation with life, to seek for some sign of God's presence, and to wait for some revelation of God's pure will, in all the events which come to you, and which you must meet in your way of life. But there is a nearer argument than this. There is clearer proof of this one true way of happy and harmonious life than even these evidences of our reason and conscience. It is shown to us—the true life, in its full strength, its noble harmony, and peace, is all revealed to us—so that a little child can respond to it, and men own its divine mastery, in the Christ of these Gospels. That was the life of perfect reconciliation with the world. There the flesh and the spirit, there the world and the soul, there the inevitableness of duty and of death, and the freedom of a Son in the Father's house, were perfectly at one, and never was there a moment's rift in the music of that life, and all was one triumph and glory of man in God. When Jesus was only twelve years old,— before that age our wills have fallen out with duty, and we have begun to tug at life's restraints,—Jesus was found in the Temple, and in his boyhood he made that memorable answer which with other but half-understood sayings of the child Jesus his mother kept in her heart: "Wist ye not that I must be in my Father's house?" Did you not know that I must be amid the things of my Father? What *must* be as his duty and his ministry was already Jesus' will of life. "I must" and "I will" strike one note in his diviner speech. When he said, "I must be about my Father's business," it was with no cheerless tone, with no heartless voice of resignation. It was his meat to do the will of Him that sent him. Knowing this world to be God's world, and perceiving life in it to be God's will, what he must do was what he would do, and every necessity of his ministry was welcome as a messenger from God's presence. The tragic inevitableness of his life—that dark shadow which he saw stealing over his path long before the disciples noticed any sign of its approach—the need of his sufferings and death, which even when he went down his trial-way they could not understand or believe—the cruel necessity of his betrayal, and the crucifixion in a world of sin, which Jesus saw must needs be the cup which it was the Father's will not to let pass from him—all this was not enough to set his heart at strife with the way which to-day and to-morrow, and the day following, he must walk, to make him cease to call God's ordained hour, "my hour," or to go, eager and strong, to meet it. "Howbeit I must go on my way to-day and to-morrow, and the day following: for it cannot be that a prophet perish out of Jerusalem." Surely it is the same eager voice speaking now which had been heard years before in the Temple, saying, "I must be about my Father's business; only it is deeper now, and calmer in its triumph. In this obedience unto death the will of God which is to be done on earth and the will of man are one and the same pure will. Jesus going up to Jerusalem, making the great *must* of the eternal purpose of God for him his joy and victory of spirit, shows the one sure way in which every man of us may become reconciled to life; and He stands in the Temple, commanding and serene, the Example and the Lord of all obedient spirits who, in doing God's will, have found themselves ushered into an eternal power and peace.

Some of you may not see now what that meant when Jesus said so royally, "I must walk to-day and to-morrow, and the day following," and, "We go up to Jerusalem." Some may feel as yet no need of understanding how the Christ could say, "I must." And others of you, under hard trials, have been seeking in broken speech to repeat those words after Christ. None of us can yet say them perfectly. The martyr singing amid the flames, the saint of God, left alone after father, mother, husband, children, perhaps all, have been taken from her—life's many blows spent, and death only waiting for her triumph,—knows something, yet knows but in part, what Jesus the Christ knew fully and for us all, when walking in his way to-day, and to-morrow, he did God's will, and going up to Jerusalem to be crucified fulfilled the work which had been given him of the Father.

There are some present who through great troubles are trying to follow Christ in a grand Christlike manner up to Jerusalem. They are thankful that they did not wait until they had to go up to Jerusalem where they must suffer, before they had learned to walk towards their hour in some Christlike trust and peace of God. It is hard if we have to be in the way towards great duties and great troubles, and at the same time have to learn in what spirit only they can be met. Jesus might never have been able to say for a world's salvation, as he drank the cup, "Not as I will, but as thou wilt," had he not been led of God to say when he was twelve years old, "I must be about my Father's business."

Others of you have not yet felt deeply the need of religious reconciliation with life through God? Very well; but you have needed it, and you do need it, although you may not yet see it or own it. Dissatisfaction with things around us begins earlier than most of us can remember. Youth is always wanting a larger objective,—something it would love to do. And young persons not infrequently find themselves in what for want of more definite self-knowledge they call "a state of mind." You will never get to the root of that state of mind until you reach down to religion. You may put your discontent from you, reason it away, or laugh it down, or dance it off for the hour; but the root of all dissatisfaction and discontent with self, and with one's surroundings and with one's prospects, never can be reached until we go down to the will of God in our soul's birth and our soul's mission, and make the discovery of that will for us, and the doing it, our chief aim and hope. No change in life's circumstances, no larger work, no happier outlook, will be enough. We ourselves need to be born again; it is not our outward life that needs to be refashioned. There are young men who occasionally attend church, who are disgusted with certain ways of the world which they know, who perhaps have not always been the best that they should have been, and who have times of serious thought. They know that they cannot escape from any of the great commandments of a moral universe. In the laws of things some "You must," stands written over against every "I will" of untruth, or unholy lust. You must reap what you sow; you must suffer for every wrong deed; you must be judged by what you are. All of us at times have realized this. Whenever we really think of it we know it. Yet there is something more, something nobler than fear of consequences, or dread of death and hell, in our hours of conscience and our moments of inward vision of better things. It is a time of the Spirit of God, whenever we become discontented with our lives, dissatisfied with ourselves. It is a great thing for us, and an opportunity of eternal life, whenever something which we see we ought to do, which we feel we must be, becomes full of attractive power over us; when the thought of it, though we keep putting it off, will as often come back to us, and our hearts begin to feel the spell of it; when though we turn our thoughts from it and would deny it, we find it there waiting again to greet and to reprove us at our first quiet moment; when in the silence of the night it haunts our last waking thoughts, and, when we awake, in that same thought we are still with God.

You know some of you what I mean. It has been your experience of religion. It is a genuine experience of religion so far as it goes. And when you submit to it, surrender to it, with an utter abandon of soul give up all to it, then its hour of blessing has come. When God says in your reason and your conscience, " You must," and in your heart you answer, " I will," the secret of life is opened—the true life of reconciliation is begun—religion has ceased to be a duty and become a delight. Although in feeble stammering tones, and as children having many things to learn, yet you have begun to say in the name of Christ, " I came forth from the Father," " I seek not mine own will, but the will of the Father that sent me;" and, " I go to the Father."

XI.

THE GLORIFICATION OF LIFE.

"Then I said, I have labored in vain, I have spent my strength for nought, and in vain: yet surely my judgment is with the Lord, and my work with my God."—Is. xlix. 4.

THIS is a small world, and a human life occupies a very little space in it. This earth affords to man a mere foothold upon space, and each generation can cling to it but for an hour. Only a speck of matter upon the infinite expanse—as a mere boat upon the great ocean—is this world upon which the generations of men are crowded. You and I are insignificant. All the stars of heaven prove our littleness. The infinite mystery of the night, as we are wrapt about by the heavens and their silences, humbles our pride in our achievement of a day. "What is man, that thou art mindful of him? and the son of man, that thou visitest him?" Even if we put all outlying space from our thought, and would live upon our little world as though it were the universe, we are forced again to acknowledge our insignificance by the shortness of the time allotted to us on earth. We do not live long enough to achieve the lives dreamed of in our youth. We die with our work undone. Our lives are not necessary to the world. Some one is always waiting for our place. There are no vacant places in history, and there are so many of us. Humanity, the mother of us all, has more life and power always to bestow than there seems to be room enough upon this earth to receive. No life reaches far into the world's future. We soon shall be forgotten, as our fathers before us. Our children will mourn us awhile after we are gone, but they will live equal to their work without us. The tree by your door has longer life than yours; the rock over which you climb exulting, was there ages before you stood upon it, and will be there ages after you are gone. And I said, "I have labored in vain, I have spent my strength for nought, and in vain." Who of us at times, when we have felt our insignificance and the littleness of our lives here, has not said something like that? Even the greatest of men are but for their hour. You look out upon the ocean, and the waves flowing in catch the sunshine each for its little moment of iridescence, and if some wave far away, rising above others, flashes in your eye, you look again, and it too has sunk into the common, lustreless flood of water. This reflection of our earthly littleness, and our human insignificance, haunts our modern consciousness of life. Our science teaches it, and our literature reflects it, and enthusiasm dies beneath it. What is it to be a man? What is it to live? Nothing great. Nothing enduring. Only a few years' consciousness of the infinitely small. And with this sense of our earthly insignificance there comes also a strange sense of isolation and loneliness. It seems as though in our human littleness, and the briefness of our period here, we were separated from the great sum of things, and cut off from the glory of the whole creation. There are within us subtle sympathies of soul which seem to bind us with universal nature, and to make us conscious parts of the divine whole of things; and this little atom of a world, upon which we ride, holds us aloof from the celestial spaces, and death soon breaks all personal union even with human life and destiny. There is something profoundly unnatural, something contrary to our inner sense of life, in this felt isolation of our earth from the heavens, and this loneliness of our life upon it. Our personal, conscious life of thought and love seems to be a brief emergence into some larger and diviner element of existence than we can measure. They tell us that the meteors which appear in our November skies are isolated little bodies, some of them probably no larger than a cherry-stone, which have been traversing space in darkness and separation, many of them computed to be over two hundred miles apart, isolated, cold, lifeless atoms of matter; and at length, when their hour is come, they enter our atmosphere, and in our air they flash for an instant into brightness, are seen for a moment of glory, and then are dissolved forever. Are the souls of men, we wonder, only momentary flashes of being in some spiritual element? Do our souls, coming from the unknown, kindle for an instant into consciousness, and die? Must we say of such a being, and such a life, It is nought? So Prof. Clifford thought when he wrote beforehand his own epitaph: "I was not; I lived; I loved; I am not." Yet never atom of matter, or created world, before the self-conscious soul of man, could write its own epitaph. "Man," said Pascal, "knows that he dies, and the universe knows nothing of the advantage it has over him." This knowledge which we have of death might mean more for us, if we could interpret it, than death itself. The being who can leave after him his own epitaph is able to do what no dissolving star can write upon the sky. He has some power of being, therefore, beyond the stars. And that word, "I loved," written between the words, "I was not," and "I am not," contradicts them both. For out of love preceding and eternal comes forth love; and love once born in a human heart begins to live for eternity.

In contrast to this oppressive sense of our human insignificance upon this infinitesimal earth, let us hasten to put the large and generous thought of life which glows in the consciousness of the chosen servant of God. "Then I said, I have labored in vain, I have spent my strength for nought, and in vain; yet surely my judgment is with the Lord, and my work with my God." As the servant of God man ceases to be for nought; the life of man with the Lord becomes great. In our connection with this little world-atom we are as nothing, and we die; but in our relation to the infinite God, who has room in his thought for all souls, we may possess the universe and be immortal. Man can never say, "My world," "my universe," "my truth," until he has first said, "My God." To seek to say, "My world," without saying, "My God," is sin, and Adam's fall. Only as the Servant of God, can man possess all things, and be as God.

The Servant of God in some passages of Isaiah's prophecy was probably perceived to be the personal Messiah, in whom the hope of Israel should be realized; but oftener when the prophet thought of the

Servant of God he had before his spirit the vision of a collective humanity, the redeemed people of God, the true Israel; and of this society and holy city of men he would say, "I have not labored in vain ; my right and my recompense is with my God." I want you in this connection to notice particularly this fundamental truth of the Old Testament prophecy that men together, in their collective capacity, as a society, or holy city, were looked upon as the elect Servant of God who should be glorified. You may sometimes have wondered why so little hope of personal immortality pervades the Old Testament. It seems to gleam from a few passages; but the thought of personal immortality in some other world was not the pervasive hope of the Old Testament. In those earlier Scriptures we read first the prophecy of the salvation of men as the people of God—the prophecy of social salvation, and social immortality. You may be surprised, if you have not thought of it, to see how the pages of prophecy grow bright with this Messianic promise of a redeemed Israel, of a coming humanity, which shall be the dwelling-place and temple of Jehovah. The individual man seems almost to be forgotten in the contemplation of the glory of Zion, the city of God. The individual man is to keep his name and have his perpetual blessing as he shares in the glory of the city of God, and its triumph becomes his. "Behold, the Lord hath proclaimed unto the end of the earth, Say ye to the daughter of Zion, Behold, thy salvation cometh; behold, his reward is with him, and his recompense before him. And they shall call them The holy people, The redeemed of the Lord;

and thou shalt be called Sought out, A city not forsaken."

Think, then, of the worth and greatness of a human life in that elect society and holy city which is the Servant of God. Think of what it would be, what power and worth, what hope, and strange, unearthly glory, would descend upon us, and wrap us around, and comprehend us all as in something divine and holy, if a single city—if this city of our homes—should begin to realize this prophetic vision of the people and city of God. If the corporate consciousness of the city should become a judgment and recompense with God; if the sense of God and His holy presence should envelop the whole city in its power, and reach every man in it, even as the morning light comes into every home; if the city should awake with God; if, throughout the day, in the mind of the city, the thought of God should have its dwelling-place, and if in the government of the people the law of God should have its throne; if some awe of the divine righteousness should pervade the business of the city, and some deep sense of divine blessedness, like a fountain of life, should well up and abound in the happiness of the city, and some greatness of the divine purpose should enlarge all the work of the city, and make the least faithfulness a service of God; if some peace of the divine eternity should rest upon all life's changes in the city, and the hope of some divine event bend over every new-made grave, and the comfort of some divine omnipresence fill as with an all-pervasive love every heart in the city that had been left in loneliness of grief;—if, in one word, a whole city, should become, what Isaiah beheld in the far future, a city of God, a Messianic city, the elect Servant of God,—think you that in that city "Sought out, A city not forsaken," any human life could seem to be a life for nought, and its labor in vain? a worthless thing to be trodden under foot, or only a moment's flash of pleasure? a life not to be prized and kept as a sacred, immortal trust? Would not every least life in a city of God, full of the consciousness of God, become a life of moral worth, a birth into an immortal consciousness, a part in some universal good, a fellowship with something celestial, an anticipation and a share in some eternal triumph and joy of life? Yet this—nothing less than this—was the revelation of human life as redeemed and glorified, in the inspiration and power of which prophets of old went before kings with the word of Jehovah, and proclaimed to the people the law of the Lord, who should redeem Israel.

Time passed; the vision of the prophet faded; the city of the scribes and Pharisees, and the Roman soldiers in the courts of the Temple, was no city of God. It had come to this, that even the chief priests in the city of David could answer, "We have no king but Cæsar." The history of the holy people seemed to be ending in this lamentation; "I have labored in vain; I have spent my strength in vain." But in the midst of the city I see one who is saying, "I and the Father are one"—"And he that sent me is with me"—"I seek not mine own will, but the will of the Father which hath sent me"—"The Father knoweth me and I know the Father." I see One walking in a strange glory of divinity among men, wrapt in an unearthly consciousness of God, standing in the midst of the rulers and speaking in the Temple as though the Infinite and Holy God from beyond the stars were present filling his woes against men's cruel falsehoods with an eternal significance, and sounding, also, from the heavens of His love, in that voice of the Son of God, His eternal word of forgiveness and of promise. I see One whom the people in their sins cannot understand, whom the powers of this world hate with a deadly hatred, whom a little company of timid followers look upon with a dazed and confused expectancy—Himself serene as a star of heaven, and his face luminous with a divine consciousness—all his judgment and his work with God—I see Him led from Pilate's seat bearing a cross, crucified between two thieves, and in the last moment of man's cruel mockery, and death's relentless grasp, saying still " My God," and, " Father, into thy hands I commend my spirit." I see One risen from the dead, appearing in the garden, still human, yet looking beyond Mary's eager adoration to the glory which he had with the Father into which he shall ascend; I see One who was crucified and buried, who appears in the midst of the disciples, bearing only the marks of his sufferings, and coming in the peace of eternity to the friends among whom he had suffered; I see One who came from God, and who had kept his divine Sonship unbroken through a life of temptation and in death, who had known God and was known of God, and whom no man had understood or can yet understand, because no man has so lived with God and God in him, I behold Him—his sufferings over and the days of his humiliation ended—bidding farewell to this little world upon which he had manifested the glory of the Highest, and from this earth, which seems to us so separate and so distant from all celestial realms, stepping into the unseen and the heavenly from that mountain-top as though it were but a moment's distance between the two, ascending into the glory which he had with God from the beginning even while the disciples stood gazing up into heaven! And from the eternal Presence, into which the Lord has vanished, comes to all the generations his word of power, " Lo, I am with you alway, even unto the end of the world."

Is the city of God a prophet's vision, the far vision still of the disciple who saw it descending from God, having the glory of God? But the realization of God upon this earth in the person of Jesus Christ is no future vision, and no vain dream. Christ was here upon this little earth in the presence and the power of God. It remains a most significant and indisputable fact of our human history that the God-man was here, that his life from beginning to end was one continuous and realized presence of God on earth. When I may deny the sun in the sky, I may deny that there has shone upon humanity a spirit all luminous with God. I do not believe it simply because disciples of old saw it, and were made new men by it, and bare witness of it; I believe it because the light of it is still in our skies. I believe it because I see it shining still in a world's thought, life-giving in our human experience, and bringing to us in our darkness and our selfishness a light, and love, and glory, in which our hearts may

The Glorification of Life. 139

become all aglow with such sense of God, and thought of heaven, as men without Christ never had, or can have; I see it, Christ's own light of God, falling upon the characters of men and women, and transfiguring them with a heavenly charity, and still the evidence of it lies over the whole Christian world, as the evidence of the sun lies upon the ripening fields. I believe that, "There was the true light, even the light which lighteth every man, coming into the world."

In what has just been said is contained the answer to that question of real life which often presses upon our spirits: How can I rise above this daily insignificance of my life? How can common life among common things become glorious in my eyes? We may begin in Isaiah's way. We may seek to dignify life by making it God's service. We may labor and pray to make our city, by all good deeds, and practical philanthropy, a city Sought out, and a city not forsaken. Every moral act is contact of the human will with God's pure will. Every good deed is a point of connection between a human life and the Eternal righteousness. Every time a man does the true, right, generous thing, he proclaims himself thereby to be more than a soulless body upon a Godless earth. Everything good and beautiful is of the celestial order, and bears witness to it; everything wrong and impure is of this earth earthy. The living God is present in conscience, and every sin is a fearful thing. Let the presence of God be felt in a city, and whither could its sin flee from that presence? Let the sins of a city come out from their darkness and corruption and be judged before the brightness of Jehovah's presence. Those frauds and deceits; those false promises and bitter words; all that uncharitableness and hatefulness; that slander and lie; that overreaching and contempt of the rights of a man; that conscienceless competition; that fraudulent custom of the trade; that shiftless piece of work; that wretched selfishness in the home; that neglect of common humanity; that petty pride, and most worthless self-sufficiency;—let them come forth, and all those dark deeds, those cruel passions of men, and shameful betrayals, and wrongs of women and of children,—let them come forth from the hiding places of the city, from the stores and the homes, yes and from the secret thoughts of our hearts,—let them come forth for judgment before the living God, whose holiness is as a consuming fire. They shall be brought to nought by the manifestation of his coming. We cannot escape from his presence. He is in the heavens, and on the earth, in the city, and in the conscience and the soul of every man. Our life is bound up with God's, and our right and our work is with God.

Thus, I would say, we may rightly begin the ennobling and glorifying of life in Israel's way of realizing Jehovah's presence. And we need a revival of the righteousness of God, a revival of the Hebrew conscience, throughout this land. But we may go also beyond Isaiah, and find God very present to us through Christ. After he had so personally and so fully realized God's presence and love on earth, Christ promised to send the Holy Ghost. And now in all the Christian life and thought of our world the Holy Spirit is working. Think the most Christian thought you can; cherish the most Christian feeling to which your heart can expand; go, do the most Christian thing you can conceive, and you will be nearest God, you will have most of God, your work will be with God. You will be in Christ's name the Servant with God; and in that service of thought or conduct you will know God, and be known of God. For the manifestation of the Lord's presence is all about us, to be found and known in everything Christian. In discipleship of the Son of God there opens for us the Holy Presence of God. Think of that wonderful prayer of Christ for all who should believe on his name:—"And the glory which thou has given me I have given unto them; that they may be one, even as we are one; I in them, and thou in me, that they may be perfected into one." He dwelt in the glory of God. Into that glory he would take our lives. Of that glory which he had with the Father he would have our lives receive.

Would that we knew more of this. Would that we had about us and in us more of this divine glorification of human life. For it is something for here and now, for to-day and to-morrow, and every hour,—this diviner consciousness and joy of a soul. There have been times when even though we have made little profession of religion, or pretense of spirituality, we have had something of this diviner consciousness of life. What was that grand sense of danger braved and duty done, but a leaping up of the spirit within us into the strength of the Eternal God? What was that strange peace and comfort, in that extreme hour of sorrow, but the descent upon us of diviner mercy than we knew? What is conscience but God's own voice? What is love but a ray of God's blessedness? What is true thought but the image of God reflecting the mind of its Maker? What is honest doubt but the spirit which is in man seeking for the divine Spirit in the universe without? We want more real religion, more sense of God around our little life. There is a sovereign, holy, and loving Presence all around us. As this earth lies ensphered in the all-encompassing sky, so, could we but see it, each human soul has its being, and lies embosomed in God and his eternal love. And this age has its work too with God. If from all these years of questioning and of thought one conviction has come to me stronger than another, and disclosed its power—a deeper depth beneath all doubt—it is the conviction that there is a God present upon this earth near to every one of us. There is a divine current flowing straight on through all the world-ages, a divine power still moving through our times. It is flowing through the world's thought and life—its purest and deepest thought and life. It is flowing beneath all churches, lifting them up to nobler things, and bearing all on to some larger service and happier Catholicity. Let us throw ourselves unreservedly into the full current and power of God's love. Let us have hearts to feel his presence. Let us have willing minds to perceive the movings of his Spirit. Let us have loving thoughts to follow the outgoings of God's grace among men. Let us not wish to hold ourselves aloof from God. Let us give up everything that would keep us apart from this diviner sense and fellowship of life. Let us leave our work with God, and dwell in the hope of the glory of

God. And when the light fails, and faith grows dim, and we know nothing but our littleness, our loneliness, and our mortality, O then let us trust with a simple and a perfect trust the Son of God who in our humanity, and for us, knew the Father, and was known of God.

XII.

A REAL SENSE OF SIN.—A LENTEN SERMON.

"And the son said unto him, Father, I have sinned against heaven, and in thy sight: I am no more worthy to be called thy son."—LUKE xv. 21.

THE observance of a season of fasting and prayer before the return of the day of the resurrection, was a custom which grew spontaneously out of the Christian consciousness of the primitive Church; and by one of those conserving providences which treasure up in Christian history what is good for man, it happens that this ancient testimony of the early Church to the sufferings and death of its Lord has survived centuries of change, and still has sufficient power to cause a social hush throughout the Christian world. In our liberty of conscience the martyrs and saints of the first Christian centuries still rule us from their graves. But in the passion and temptation of our world Christians cannot afford to wear any formal habit, or to cling to anything fictitious in religious experience. Life is bringing everything religious to the test of reality. Our spiritual experiences must be honest, or they cannot claim to be religious. No secondhand religion will answer the uses of our times. Genuineness is the first necessity of the living Church. Men are not to be guided through the straits of to-day by echoes of the voices of yesterday. Christians must still speak what they have seen and

A Real Sense of Sin. 145

do know, if they are to have apostolic success in casting out the sins of men. Religious genuineness is particularly desirable in all penitential expressions. An unreal and imitated sense of sin enervates character. A fictitious, theological sense of sin, rather than a vital, moral conviction of it, has produced no little unconscious Jesuitism in Protestant communions. Genuine penitence, on the contrary, is the soil from which all virtue may spring.

I wish, accordingly, to improve this first Sunday in Lent by leaving in the thoughts of all of you, if possible, this question:—What morally real thing for us corresponds to the once familiar phrase, a conviction of sin?

I think we are exposed to the temptation of religious fictitiousness in our use of penitential language. We are liable to use forms of abject confession from habit, or from a sense of duty, when there may be little truth corresponding to such expressions in our sense of life and happiness. For fear lest some constituent element of religious experience common to our fathers may be fading out from our piety, we seek to reproduce tones and colors of experience which do not altogether harmonize with the type and habit of religious devotion most commonly produced by the Holy Spirit in our churches. Occasionally individuals among us may with inward sincerity restore forms of spiritual experience which were familiar under other conditions of religious thought and life; but such persons seem now to be the exceptions rather than the rule. I noticed, for example, in reading the other evening, some phrases in which Oliver Cromwell in his letters describes his sense of personal unworthiness, and his dwelling in Meshec, as well as the allusion which he made to the experience of vanity and the carnal mind, through which his young daughter was being led in the mercy of God, and the account also of the searchings of conscience, and the weeping even of the leaders of the Parliamentary Army in preparation for their decision to fight in their second civil war. Those expressions of Oliver Cromwell and his soldiers have in them a nerve and vigor which indicate their moral genuineness; but if this morning I should read a collection of similar phrases from the passages of religious biography, I doubt if they would seem altogether natural and real even to many truly humble and devout persons in a modern congregation. At least we should have to interpret them by other feelings and experiences to fill them with present moral meanings.

Now there are two ways in which we may look at this obvious state of things. We may say, men ought to have such convictions of sin, such sense of the utter wretchedness of man, as once characterized profound religious experience; and, therefore, we will continue using the forms of that experience, and preaching the doctrines under which that experience grew; and we will resist as a defection from the faith once delivered to the saints of the middle ages any, even the slightest, deviation from those doctrines, or from that type of religious experience. The chief difficulty with this method of dealing with the fact is that it attempts the impossible. For we are all of us in these matters under a higher Power, and Providence creates for us the spiritual conditions of our times. We may think that the general religious temper of some former age was better than ours; but we have to breathe the religious atmosphere which the Spirit, that bloweth where it listeth, provides in our times, and Christian wisdom consists always in making the best of present providential conditions. The atmosphere of the carboniferous age was doubtless more favorable than that of the present day for the formation of the vegetable growths which have been left for our use in the great coal beds; but our present atmosphere is the air provided for our life,—and, indeed, there are more singing birds in it. We should gain nothing by bringing back, if we could, the carboniferous age of theology —the age of the deposit of the great confessions;— our duty is to make the most profitable use of these results of the past life of the Church, and let Christion faith grow now, as best it may, according to its present spiritual environment.

The other, and better way, therefore, of regarding this matter, is to accept thankfully and hopefully our present religious conditions, and then to watch and to pray, that we may conform our inward experiences to the best and the truest which is now in the providence of God actually possible to us.

The question with which we started reduces itself, accordingly, to this: Without attempting to reproduce exactly former religious experiences, what real sense of sin should I gain under the circumstances of my own life? In this effort to find further and helpful answer to this question, I would ask attention to the following considerations:—

First, Our conviction of sin will correspond to our

idea of God. In other words what we may think of ourselves, and of our sinfulness, will run parallel with our thought of God and his relation to us. If a man, for example, habitually thinks of his God as only an impassive nature, or thoughtless Power, who cares for none of these things, his corresponding sense of human sinfulness will not rise above a conviction of human failure and misfortune. This proposition that our sense of sin and our idea of God go together, is so plain, that, without arguing it, I pass to the next statement necessary to clear up this subject.

Secondly, We cannot hold one conception of God, and attach to it a conviction of sin which belongs to another conception of God. We cannot retain a religious feeling or experience which is the reflex of one predominant conception of God, if we have habitually in our mind a different thought of God. For example, when St. Augustine ceased to think of this world as under the dominion of two powers of good and evil, and believed in one true God, he saw the sins of his youth in altogether a new light. So as we change, or clarify, or Christianize, our thought of God, our religious feelings will naturally follow that change, and our sense of sin, if it be genuine, will correspond to our thought of what God is, and of what we are towards God. Yet just at this point we are apt to fall into religious fictitiousness. We may not discern how great has been the change which has come over men's thoughts concerning God, and so vainly strive to force ourselves into emotions and convictions which were true to former ideas of God, but which are not true to our prevalent thought of God.

This brings me to a third statement which I will take just time enough to render intelligible, viz.: there was once a prevalent thought of God, which may broadly be defined as the Latin theology, and corresponding to that theology there was cultivated a peculiar conviction of sin. After the Gospel had become domesticated upon this earth, and the apostles had left the new heavenly faith to become naturalized in the thoughts and customs of the world, the Greek mind took Christianity to itself. And the Greek mind seized strongly upon the truth of the divine naturalness of Christ, of the fitness of the Gospel to human nature, of the oneness of God and man in the incarnation. The Nicene Creed marks that faith of the ancient church. Then the Roman mind appropriated Christianity. And Christian Rome was nothing, if not imperial. Rome made of the Gospel a new law for the nations. Hence Latin theology was moulded in the idea of God's sovereignty. Augustine's theology had in it permanent truths, which profound religious experience will still recognize; but it was formed and fashioned as a theology for a church which was commissioned to rule men. Bring the theology of Roman scholasticism into comparison with the parable of the prodigal son, and its distinctive character becomes evident at a glance. The Father becomes an Emperor; and he is not present every day in the common life of the household, personally managing its affairs, but he dwells withdrawn in august state upon his throne, and the Church as chief servant becomes the lord of the house. The prodigal must return to the chief servant, and receive indulgence through him.

Calvinism revolted from this subjection to the church and its hierarchy, and brought every individual soul face to face with God. But Calvinism retained the Latin idea of Christianity as a divine statecraft. Calvin's idea of God shows still the lines of Augustine's Latin mould in which it was cast. To God the Sovereign Ruler, whose law had been broken, comes man the sinner, to be elected, or to be reprobated, according to God's good pleasure. The Calvinistic idea of God exalted His wisdom and His holiness; but the Calvinistic theology was nothing, if not imperial. We should acknowledge that there was a providence in this subjection of the modern nations at their birth to an imperial theology. Man needs to be mastered by the sovereignty of God before he is ready for deeper and kindlier revelations of the Spirit.

Such then, broadly speaking, was the Latin thought of God. And my present point is, that this thought was accompanied by its corresponding sense of sin in the minds of the men who held it. They looked up into the heavens, and saw, holding the stars in his hand, an All-wise and Omnipotent Ruler, whose law man had broken, and under whose condemnation the whole guilty world was lying in its sin. They believed that all souls had had their day of probation in Adam, and all generations were bound together in one common disobedience and original sin, and are justly exposed to the wrath of God. They read the Gospels under that conception of God's sovereign holiness, and they dared trust Christ enough to believe that in the secret and gracious counsels of God his sufferings would be sufficient atonement for the elect. No wonder that under such conceptions of God's supreme Will, and the awful majesty of the divine law, the hearts of men smote within them, that even young children, on their way to the Cross of him who once took infants from their mothers' arms and blessed them, must be made to pass through horrors of contrition like the torments of the damned; and that poor Cowper "from a maniac's tongue" sent up the cry, "Forsaken!" And when God's love prevailed, as it often did in men's thought of their redemption, still their experience of grace was darkened by a deep sense of the broken law and the utter depravity of man's nature.

Now if we would reproduce in our churches exactly that religious experience, and particularly its conviction of sin, we must reproduce the conditions of thought and life in the world under which that experience was once genuine and true. But we cannot do that, for, fourthly, during the past hundred years, throughout the Christian world, a change has been coming over men's thought of God.

What has happened is this: the sun has been rising, and the shadow of Rome has been shortening over the modern Christian world. And particularly, —to keep close to my present subject,—the world's thought of its God has been growing more Christlike. We have not been losing utterly the truth that there is a divine law in the universe. Indeed physical science, with its exaltation of law, and its stern creed of heredity, has been helping us keep in mind what was true in the Calvinistic conception of the infrustrable divine decrees. There is a will of God to be done in all the processes of life, and there is a sovereign order of the Creator in the heavens. But gradually, and almost without observation, our conception of God's nature and His sovereignty has been gaining a more Christian tone and color. A purer and warmer light glows through our thought of God. What Christ was seen by the disciples to be, that we dare believe God is essentially and eternally. Anything Christlike is absolutely to be trusted. The Word was made flesh. Christ is the revelation of God. All our thoughts of God are to be formed and fashioned, not in the type of natural law, nor in the mould of any human government, nor in the image of Cæsar, but after the likeness of Christ, who is the express image of the Father's person. Our God is exalted in the heavens, the Lord of hosts; yet He is a sovereign, holy, and loving presence in this world, and there are not two kingdoms, one of nature and the other of grace, but there is one Divine revelation through all;—God is in nature, and nature is God's, and divine things are also most natural, and most human, for Creator and creation are one in Christ, the incarnate Word.

We now draw near the answer for which these remarks have been preparatory. Corresponding to this increasing Christian sense of God there is a conviction of sin which we may realize. We are to gain it simply by coming into the Light of Christ's character in its adorable revelation of God, and seeing ourselves in that Light. God is all around us, a holy, sovereign, loving Presence; we have in all things to do with that One omnipresent, Christlike Character. Everything sinful, the least wrong, touches and jars against the pure divinity around us; it is contrary to God in Christ, contrary to the infinite Christlikeness of God. There is, indeed, a divine order of the world, a law of righteousness in nature, and in the life of man. And the prodigal's sin was against heaven;—sin is against the whole celestial order of being. But this is not all. We do not reach the truest and most convincing experience of sin until we have said, "Father, I have sinned against thee!" It is not simply, when we sin, that we are breaking a law, and exposing ourselves to punishment; it is more like breaking the trust of a friend. We are in the pure and friendly presence of the living God. Sin wounds that. Sin is the prodigal's wrong against the Father. Feel that divine fatherhood, feel that all-encompassing divine friendship, and in its presence you would not think again that anxious, loveless, jealous thought. We would not speak that uncharitable word in the hearing of such a God as Christ reveals. You cannot consent to that untruth; you cannot refuse that duty; you must not yield to that temptation, if you realize the presence of the Spirit of Christ round about you;—the disciples fell upon their faces and worshipped, when the transfiguring light of God's presence shone from the face, and the very raiment of Christ upon that holy mount.

Corresponding also to this increasing sense of God in his Christlike presence around our thoughts and ways, there will spring up within us a growing sense of the moral hatefulness of particular sins. There is a Christlike scorn to be cherished for things contemptible. To the cowardly scribes and Pharisees, hypocrites, in our own thoughts we must learn to say, and mean it,—Woe be unto you! We have a personal example of God's rectitude by which to measure our conduct. Take the Sermon on the Mount in your heart down the street with you, and let it reveal to you what the sin of the world is. Or come, take the cup of the communion of Christ, and at the Lord's table, while we receive the forgiveness of sin, let us understand what thoughts of our hearts have been with the multitude who cried, "Crucify him." How should I remember that denial of duty? how think of that sin? How did Peter feel when suddenly, while he was cowering in that angry crowd, he saw Jesus' eye quietly resting upon him? "And the Lord turned, and looked upon Peter. . . . And Peter remembered. . . . And he went out and wept bitterly."

Again, in consonance with this increasing sense of God's adorable Christlikeness there springs up a strong sense of the worth of character. We want character more than anything else. We want not this or that virtue merely, but character equal to all duty and trial; we want character worthy of all admiration; we want character which can never be put to shame; we want character so strong, clear, and pure, that God himself can look upon it and be pleased. We look at Jesus Christ, and if we once see him as he is, we must pray ever afterwards for character—more character and nobler than we have ever attained in our broken lives. We can never be satisfied without Christlike character. Moreover, this perception of perfect character and our admiration of it in Christ, discloses to us our deepest need of reconciliation. At the bottom of our hearts, at the spring of our wills, we need to become at one with such a God. Our God as revealed in Christ is too noble, too righteous, too just, too attractive and adorable, for us not to wish to be at one in our inmost being with such infinite Christlikeness. And we see and feel how our lives do not yet fit into that divine element of our being. Our characters, all around their edges, are ragged, and broken, and at heart they do not rest quietly in God. They must be poised and centered upon that pure will of God, and be rounded and fitted to that perfection. There can be no real peace for us, until our souls become fitted to the divine element in which they were made to have their being. There is no true, lasting reconciliation with life possible for us, except through reconciliation with God.

Once having seen and felt this divine Christlikeness to which human hearts are made to correspond, we shall know what alienation from God our sin is, and we shall turn with a strong repentance from all our littleness, selfishness, and unworthiness. "Ye therefore shall be perfect, as your heavenly Father is perfect." That convinces us of sin. The spell of an infinite attraction has been laid upon us. Conscience within us has seen that gracious possibility of character, and leaped for joy. Desert it, choose lower good, be content with a fragmentary virtue, and conscience would become an avenging torment. Follow it, and conscience by its very rebukes becomes a herald of happiness. For "every man that hath this hope in him purifieth himself, even as he is pure."

Along lines of experience like these we may gain for ourselves, and in accordance with our present spiritual conditions of life, genuine and profitable conviction of sin. And to such penitence the word of forgiveness is ever spoken, and from it ascends the acceptable prayer of the new life.

XIII.

PERSONAL POWER.

"Jesus therefore walked no more openly among the Jews, but departed thence into the country near to the wilderness, into a city called Ephraim; and there he tarried with the disciples."—JOHN xi. 54.

DURING the latter part of February, or early in March, Jesus withdrew from Jerusalem, and retired with his disciples to a solitary place in the wild, hill-country to the North East of Jerusalem. A few days before the seventh of April—the day upon which that year the feast of the passover fell,—Jesus left Ephraim, and to the amazement and fear of his disciples went before them in the way which led up to Jerusalem. Thus for several weeks, and at this time of the year, Jesus, as John tells us, tarried with the disciples at Ephraim. His enemies did not know where he was; he did not appear in the midst of the multitude in the temple; for a few quiet weeks he was doing personal work with his disciples.

It is helpful to us, whenever the Gospel narratives permit it, to associate Jesus' words and deeds with particular days or seasons of the year. It serves to make Jesus' wonderful life more real and present to us to think, What was the Lord doing this very day? What words did he speak at this time? During this season of our year, at this time which the Christian world is consecrating more and more generally to religious thought and works of repentance, Jesus had withdrawn from the crowds of the great cities, and was tarrying with his disciples at Ephraim.

Yet never since Jesus began to go about doing good, had there been more need of his works of mercy. There were many lepers besides those wandering, God-forsaken, upon the borders of Samaria. There were still sick folk enough to be healed in Capernaum. There were devils to be cast out from degraded souls in the towns and cities of Judea. The common people were suffering under burdens too heavy to be borne, which the ruling classes had bound upon them. It was not because the world was not waiting for Jesus' presence in it that he tarried some five weeks with his disciples at Ephraim. There was a will of God for Jesus, and a work also for his disciples, to be done in those quiet days at Ephraim. Doubtless that season was for Jesus himself a preparation for his hour. But Jesus did not depart to Ephraim for himself alone; he tarried there with his disciples. Those disciples were strong, eager men, who felt keenly the evils of their times; they were men of the people who knew how much wrong there was in the towns of Judea, and how the populace throughout Galilee needed a Messiah;—impetuous men like Peter, quick to draw the sword; sons of thunder, like James and John; and also that cold, calculating soul called Judas, who was "on the make" even in the Lord's company, and who was impatient to make more from the revolution which he thought was coming. These twelve disciples Jesus took with him, and kept quietly with him, while he tarried in Ephraim. Judas must have found it a dull town; and, often the boisterous waves of Galilee may have leaped up in Peter's memory, and he would think of the crowds waiting for his Master on the shore; but Jesus tarried with the disciples at Ephraim.

That time was for them an opportunity of personal concentration. It was a preparation for their future apostleship. They might gain personal power in those weeks. The Lord was with them to teach them his truth. His example laid its spell upon their spirits. His light was shining into their inmost souls, and revealing them to themselves. His peace kept them in its perfect patience. This, accordingly, is the lesson of our text for us at this time. In the Christian life, and for it, there is to be a preparation of personal power. We need to gather personal force for life. In order that the Christian disciple may become a Christian apostle he is to gain through companionship with Christ personal concentration and power.

In speaking further of this personal preparation and power for our lives, let me remind you of the danger of our becoming distracted, and almost losing our souls, among the many things which we want to do, or which we think ought to be done. I do not refer merely to the innumerable little things among which our lives may seem to run out into nothingness, as some rivers are lost in the sands; nor do I have in mind chiefly that absorbing necessity of business in which the heart of a man's life may be in danger of becoming sucked dry. I am speaking more especially of the services which Christians are called upon to render, the kindly, helpful things which some one must be always doing, if people are to be held up, and society is not to slip backwards. The demands upon the benevolence, and the helpful powers, of the Church have been steadily increasing for a hundred years. When were there ever more useful things needing to be done right off than there are to-day? When did liberal and large-minded Christian men and women ever have so many opportunities to do good, and to do a great deal of good, as the providences of God are now affording? Literally the field now is the world. Our Christianity in sober truth has the opportunity now to overcome evil with good throughout the whole world. The twelve of old began to bear witness to their Lord at Jerusalem; and then providence led the way to Antioch, and opened Asia Minor, and Macedonia, and continued enlarging the scope of their possible service, until we find Peter writing to the Dispersion in several countries, and one brave Apostle had made the discovery that the Gospel was for all the Gentiles. That providence which enlarged the horizon of the Apostles, has continued expanding the task of Christianity, and by calls for men, and drafts upon our property, from all quarters, in the name of the Lord, we are taught that God loves the world, and our Christ is for all men. Or consider the task laid upon our Christianity within the limits of a single city. We may not always realize it, but it is a work set by the providence of God before the doors of every church, and a good waiting to be done around all Christian homes. The work of making a single city righteous, pure, happy, like the city of God, might task the resources of angels. Yet that city, and nothing less than that city of God, is the ideal of the true Church of Christ. In order to the next possible approximation towards that Christian ideal how many helpful things, and true things, and strong things, need to be done, and as soon as possible! Still coiled beneath our civilization is the serpent whose head must be bruised by the heel of our Christianity. We all know, or may know, men and women, boys and girls, who need daily to be helped to good, useful, and honorable lives. And confronting the Church all the while is the popular atheism— the dull, despairing, sometimes revengeful feeling that the Christian's God has gone on a far journey, and does not care for poor needlewomen, or mind day-laborers. There is, also, that other atheism in our hearts, which leaves us imagining that it is practically impossible for our Christ to do as much for many other people, or for nobody's children, as he has done for us and our children. And here, in the very heart of a city, upon whose streets during a single year representatives of eighteen or twenty different nationalities have been met, stands a house of God, a Puritan meeting-house, whose foundations were laid by men who believed with all their might in the city of God, and who crossed the seas in search of it; and all this fixed capital of religion is held by Christians as a sacred trust in the name of the Lord, every pew and pew door of it; and as faithful stewards we would not deny our obligation to put this fixed capital of religion, this whole religious *plant*, to the largest profits, and to use it not for our own edification merely, and our children's, but for the good of the whole community, and with some wise prevision of the kind of society, law-abiding and free, or Godless and forsaken, in which we would have our children and children's children receive hereafter their inheritance from us. Such is the briefest outline or suggestion of the good works to which our Christian faith is pledged.

Yet notwithstanding all the work needing to be done, Jesus departed with his disciples to Ephraim. In those hours when the disciples tarried with Jesus in some place near the wilderness, a deep personal work was going on. Their lives during those quiet, intense days, instead of expanding outwardly, were folded in upon themselves. It was a season for them of self-concentration in the presence of their Lord. While the world was perishing in its sins, Jesus took time to deepen and to intensify the personal life of his disciples before he sent them forth finally into the world as his apostles. Renewed and inspired personalities were to be the Lord's means of grace to the world. The method of Christianity is personal influence. The world is not to be saved by institutionalism. Human society is to be redeemed and glorified by the personal lives, full of light and warmth, which shall strike through and illumine it. Divine grace is not an impersonal property—a sacramental magic, or a governmental provision—an intermediate something between the soul of man and the Spirit of God; it is the love of God concentrated and incarnate in the Person of Jesus Christ, and from him working through his disciples as the living and personal power of the new life of redemption. More than anything else, essentially and vitally, Christianity is the personal influence of Jesus—his continual personal influence, always coming into human life—the Light of the world caught and reflected by each succeeding generation, glowing through thousands of lives that kindle in its beams, and becoming, through the multitude of these, the diffused radiance of a world's civilization. If we imagine that we can substitute anything else for this personal influence of Jesus we shall fail. Unless we can have among us men who have tarried with the Lord at Ephraim long enough to become personal centers and forces of righteousness and truth, we shall make only a formal and fruitless thing of all our charities and all our churches. Yet just this truth that the power of the Gospel lies in the personalities which it seizes upon, and inspires, we are in danger of losing sight of in the multiplicity of our agencies for doing good in the world. Jesus Christ made men before he made the church. Jesus created and concentrated strong, personal forces among his personal followers, before he gave to the disciples the cup of communion, and ordained them as his apostles to gather congregations of believers in his name. In Christ's work the inspired personality came first, and afterwards the New Testament and the Church. A true communion, or saved society of men and women, was the end sought from the beginning by Him who came preaching the Gospel of the kingdom; but the method of Jesus was personal influence, and the inspiration of chosen personalities by his Spirit. The power of the Church consists in its fullness of personal forces. Your personal power for good may be multiplied many fold in the organized life of the Church; but personal powers are the vital units which, multiplied together, constitute that organic whole which is the living body of Christ.

The same remark applies as pertinently to all charitable work. Benevolence of late has been compelled to organize in the face of modern wants. Village methods do not answer city needs. Association is becoming in all large towns the approved method of charity. We form societies for almost every good work. The economic helpfulness of love in modern society lies largely in its organization; and its weakness also is there. Its power for good is increased by combination of the many in one working force; but its danger lies in the ease with which we suffer the organization to take the place of the personal influence in our good works. Many of you, very many of you, are connected with one or with several of the philanthropic and Christian societies of this city. In those organizations your personal influence may be taken up, and increased, as an integer in a multiplication table. You can do more through those societies than you could apart from them. Yes, if you are doing what you may through the organization, and not trusting the organization to do it for you. If we make charitable proxies of these societies, we may indeed help other persons to do more; but we cannot accomplish what we might, if instead of making charitable proxies of them we regard them as points of application for personal influence. If your object is to keep your benevolent society alive, you may indeed help others find opportunity of doing good through it; but if you would take that philanthropic society to which you belong and make it a means of your personal service, a point of application of your personal force to some want or sin of the city, for all the people of which Christ tasted death, then some of the greater works of faith might become possible here. But if we idly subordinate the personal to the institutional, we shall see around us anything except the Christianity of Jesus Christ. Yet that is exactly the mistake which for centuries the church made. For the personal power of Jesus, multiplied in apostolic lives, men very early began to substitute the outward power of the Church. Augustine saw the wickedness of the world, and also the power of the Roman Church to extend through the pagan world a system of compulsory baptism and education of men into Christianity. The papal power rose and fell. Then the Reformation began with a new contact of the Gospel with life through personal apostles of it. And there is no other way for Christianity to win its world-triumph than through the personal forces which it vitalizes. So long therefore as a benevolent or religious organization represents and multiplies personal service, so long it is useful; whenever it stands by its own institutional weight, and for its own sake, ceasing to be vivified and fructified with personal influences, it cumbers the ground, and should be cut down.

This principle holds true especially of the Church. So long as it is a living multiplication of the influence of Jesus through personal powers united in one body, it is an Apostolic church; but let it cease to be in any real sense a missionary church,—a point of application, that is to say, of organized personal forces to the work of the Lord,— and, however venerable its customs, or distinguished its past, or rich its inheritance of name, property, or tradition, it would fall out of the true Apostolical succession, and fail of the work for which it was ordained of God.

Jesus' tarrying with his disciples at Ephraim in the midst of the most active season of his ministry, even while the pilgrims to the feast were already seeking him in Jerusalem, contains thus a very necessary lesson for all of us who would learn how to live large and helpful lives. It is the lesson which it seems to me young men and women must learn before they ever can begin to live as they are capable of living. Our natures quickly open toward things without, and respond happily to outward impressions. We are mirrors of life, before we are makers of our lives. And some go on for years and years mirroring the world rather than making their souls. This expansiveness of mind and heart toward the world is a natural impulse, and a true impulse. But there must be also a deepening of life, a concentration of soul for life, a gathering of personal power. All serious times are hours when this outward, expansive impulse is held in check for the time by this other deeper, intensive sense of one's soul, and its vital needs. And if we should not gain clear concentration of soul in purpose, if we should fail of this deepening and inflowing from God of personal truth and power, then there would be danger that in the heat of the world, and under the glare of social life, our souls would evaporate from us into the world, and our life become indeed as a vapor that passeth away. But we cannot gather deep, vital personal power without religious experience. When the soul is thrown in upon itself, it is put back directly upon God. For at every vital centre of every living thing is God. At the springs of life is always the living God. This religious experience, this deepening and intensifying, as well as purification, of the personal life, is an experience most truly and fully to be realized in the discipleship of Jesus Christ. Let the disciple go with the Lord to Ephraim and tarry with him, and we may observe what shall surely follow. The Christ discloses to the soul its true self. He brings out from our inmost being, and sets visibly before us, even in his own image, that true, diviner self, which God thought of as possible when he created us. And the knowledge of that both convinces us of sin, and at the same time fills us with a new desire and great hope; it humbles us in a genuine repentance, and puts us upon a new life with an inspiring faith. Such an experience, call it conversion, or what you may, such a gathering of personal force for life under the personal influence of Jesus Christ, has been with many the great epoch of their years,—as a new birth of soul in the Spirit of Christ. It was their call to apostleship. That experience has put them in the succession of true and consecrated souls. Life since then may have run too much to waste; they may have been unprofitable servants; but, still kept by the grace of God within them, is that vital centre of personal good which may be quickened, and invigorated, and from which a greater devotion and happier may yet grow.

God has many Ephraims where he provides for

our tarrying with the Christ. The opportunity of soul-quickening and deepening came to some of you in the preparation to meet a new responsibility or an approaching happiness. Others have found themselves left alone with the Spirit through some disappointment. Any call of life upon us may lead us for a brief season to turn in upon ourselves, and to seek for new gathering of personal power. Or sickness may have kept some strong man for weeks from his business, taken the man bodily out of his customary surroundings, and given him time to think. He learned in that Ephraim of his soul with his Lord to measure the whole striving of his life by a juster standard, to value at their true worth whatever he has of culture, power, or money; to know himself as he stands independently of all his possessions in the sight of God. He has seen again perhaps some heavenly vision of the new man in Christ Jesus which he saw in his youth, or which years ago dawned upon him at his conversion. Let him not dare to forget again as he goes about his work what the Spirit taught him when he tarried at Ephraim. God knows every place in our lives where we had time and opportunity to be quickened, and deepened, and vitalized anew by the Spirit.

This special season of the year may prove to some such a time of the Spirit. This time of Lent gives opportunity to those who delight in life's outward happiness to come to themselves. They will enter again into that outward life with more heart, and a happier appreciation, if now their souls should deepen, and strengthen, and concentrate in the disciple's decision: from that decision as from an exhaustless motive their life might ever afterward expand, and fill its whole opportunity of good, and overflow into all the joy of the Father's house. Let the Church, tarrying with its Lord for a season, become full of the personal power of Jesus, and it might do an Apostolic work wider, farther reaching, more redemptive of the city, the country, and the world, than any of us have ever seen or known.

XIV.

THE GREAT REQUIREMENT.

"𝔄𝔫𝔡 𝔠𝔬𝔪𝔢, 𝔱𝔞𝔨𝔢 𝔲𝔭 𝔱𝔥𝔢 𝔠𝔯𝔬𝔰𝔰, 𝔞𝔫𝔡 𝔣𝔬𝔩𝔩𔬀𔬀 𝔪𝔢."—MARK X. 21.

ONE afternoon in the year 1210, as Pope Innocent III., surrounded by a sumptuous retinue of prelates, was walking on the terrace of the Lateran, a company of mendicants laid at his feet the articles of a new association. At their head was a young man who but a few years before had been foremost in every scene of merriment; he had been a "successful merchant, a gallant soldier, and one of the most popular of the sons of Assisi." But, while seeking military service and adventure, he had endured a protracted sickness; and when, upon his recovery and his return, his friends gathered at one of the gates of Assisi to welcome him, and merrily placed in his hand the sceptre of frolic, to their astonishment he remained grave in the midst of their festivities, as one not of them, and suddenly breaking loose from his companions, (so the story runs,) he proceeded to the church, and before its high altar there was witnessed a wedding which has been celebrated by Italy's great poet, and is still represented in the same Cathedral by Giotto's art; and at the wedding of St. Francis the name of the bride was *Poverty*. The solemn espousal of poverty by this youth of Assisi was no meaningless ceremony. To him the vow of his soul before that high altar meant emptied coffers, surrender of the comforts of life, patient endurance of evil, and even self-torture, and withal a love of all created things so joyous and overflowing that, as he wandered among the mountains or over the plains of Italy, he would speak of the beasts of the field as his brethren, and the twittering swallows as his little sisters. The vow of self-sacrifice, and his espousal of poverty meant the unflinching prosecution of a work of moral purification for which Europe for at least two generations was better, and the founding and resolute administration of an order of missionary monks whom, it has been justly said, the violent learned to fear, the rich to respect, and the poor to love. The command of Christ, "Come, take up the cross, and follow me," was understood by St. Francis of Assisi to mean a life given up as entirely to a noble aim as the bow gives up the swift arrow to the mark.

We read the story of St. Francis, and smile, and put it from us as a pleasing bit of medievalism. Such singular sacrifice might have place and fitness in that odd mosaic of medieval manners and life. It would not be in accordance with the sensible and soberer coloring of real life in this most prosaic of the centuries. Should the life of St. Francis be held up in the pulpit as an example for us, a comfortable and well-dressed modern Congregation would regard it as a romantic picture, and we should not think of imitating the visionary sainthood and unnatural asceticism of those spiritual heroes and heroines of the middle ages.

Nevertheless, what do these words of our Master,

concerning losing our life, and taking up the cross, mean to us?

Let us look at another picture which is not medieval, and which we cannot so easily put aside with a smile of complacent wisdom. The scene was in a city bordering on the wilderness. The time was about the year 30 of our era, and in the early Spring. One who was so human in all his sympathies, and yet so unlike all other men that he had become known as the Son of man, was in the way going up to Jerusalem. And a young ruler met him, and asked him that old and ever new question of the human soul concerning the eternal life. You have heard read this morning the account of that meeting, which made so great an impression upon the memories of all who witnessed the scene that we find it recorded in each of the three evangelists. And there may have come to us again the thought which the narrative so often has suggested, why did Jesus ask of that young Israelite a sacrifice seemingly so unnecessary? and who then can be saved? We may put the story of St. Francis from us as an idle tale; but here for us all to look upon in the Gospels is this picture of the *One Great Requirement;*—and is that only as a medieval painting to us? How shall we catch the spirit of it, and in our lives, amid present surroundings, reproduce what the Lord would have us imitate in that commandment?

My friends, we shall never understand these Gospels of the life of Christ, if we read them as the scribes read the Scriptures. We must look beyond the letter, we must enter into the spirit of that hour when Jesus stood before the young ruler, loving him, and asking of him a great requirement, or else we shall not understand what its truth for all men is, and we shall turn from it utterly, or make but caricatures of it in our poor efforts to reproduce it.

If we would rightly understand this sacred narrative, we should not regard it as a chapter of dogmatic teaching to be taken by itself, but we should look upon it as a scene from real life to be studied, and interpreted, in its time and place in the ministry of Jesus. Remember it was while he was going up to Jerusalem that the young ruler met him. Jesus was on his way to the great sacrifice. It was no common time even in the life of our Lord. His hour was at hand. Some three years before he had gone to Cana of Galilee, and blessed a wedding-feast. A few weeks before he had entered a home of sorrow, and had restored to its happy friendship the brother who had been loved and lost. He had never asked those friends of his to give up their pleasant home amid the olives of Bethany. Never had his presence hushed the song of a single pure joy of the human heart. But now the great sacrifice of the ages awaits him in the holy city. He has taken his disciples aside, and told them privately, even while the multitude are ready to shout Hosannas, that he must needs suffer. Think then, with reverent thought, what must have been the divine consciousness of Jesus when that young ruler, strong, healthful, and conscientious, but without sign upon him of sacrificial sympathies and self-denials, came to him, the Christ, on his way to the Cross. It was the sudden meeting of a conscientious and painstaking, and cold moral nature, satisfied in keeping for itself the right way to heaven, and an Incarnate Love, full of all human sympathies and inwardly aglow with the purpose of an infinite sacrifice. It was a great Character at its greatest, and before it our common rectitude in its commonest complacency. It was the supreme Incarnation of what God is, before a fair representation of what selfish man at his best may be. Christ in the clear consciousness of the Love of God stands before man in the half-hearted obedience of his conscience. It is the supernal Good dwarfing all lesser good. It is the commanding Love making all easier sacrifice seem as nothing. It is God revealing the glory of his eternal Love to man in his poor selfishness. It is the Christ in his perfect sacrifice of himself convincing you and me of sin. Never has scene like this been witnessed before or since:— The Christ from God on the way to the Cross, the ruler for a moment in his presence, meeting the great requirement of the greatest Character, and returning sad at heart to his possessions. Of how little worth those possessions seem when put in contrast with such a character. Nearly two years before a voice, not like the voice of man, had been heard giving new commandments, heralding strange blessings, and saying to the common people, "Ye therefore shall be perfect, as your heavenly Father is perfect." And to-day man at his poor best came and stood for a moment before the Christ who was walking in the consciousness of his hour which was almost come; and at that meeting of the Divine and the human that strange promise of the Sermon on the Mount became the seemingly impracticable requirement which was laid upon our common humanity by that perfect character of incarnate Love; "If thou wilt be perfect, go and sell that thou hast, and give to the poor, and thou shalt have treasure in heaven: and come and follow me."

In this passage of the Gospel we have for our imitation not the letter, but the spirit; not a specific commandment, everywhere, and under all circumstances, to be obeyed, but a Character revealing itself in its divinest power, to be chosen and loved by us, to be imitated and followed in all men's ways of life.

What do these words, Take up the cross, go, sell that thou hast, give to the poor, follow me, mean to us? That will depend upon how much perception of the real intention of Jesus we may have gained, upon how much willingness of heart we may have to perceive the true Spirit of Christ.

Let us think of this further. Should imitation of that Spirit of life as it was revealed in this impressive scene, lead us to utter abandonment of our present possessions? Would the Christ who stood in his sacrificial purpose before that good and lovable, but spiritually commonplace man, bid us remove the pictures from our homes, the cheerful fire from the hearth, and all pleasure from our hearts?

What is this Christian law of sacrifice? Is it annihilation of self? Is it "at enmity with joy"? My friends, we have indeed but little faith—not faith enough to bear the least trial, or with which to look at any death—if we have not yet learned that God is over all, God *blessed* forever, and that life, and the joy of life, is the creation's primal law, and the creation's chief end. When we say, God is the Alpha and the Omega, we confess that blessedness and not pain is the first and the last. When we believe that God in his blessedness is from eternity to eternity, we believe that Life— full, perfect life—life and not death—joy of life and not pain of death,—is the supreme law and universal good. If now we must needs know death and pain, it is because these unhappy facts have in some way found place, and become entangled, in the midst of things. They must be intermediate things, incidental, temporary, not eternal,—not the end of the creation, but only means to its end; for the beginning and the end, the first and the last, is God,—and He who is over all, is God blessed forever. Life is the Creator's law; death the creation's incident; blessedness is the supreme good, sacrifice the means to the final good. The Christ must needs suffer, not forever, but once for all; and in the same announcement it was foretold that he should be crucified, and that he should rise again. That supernal Character, the Incarnation of the Love of God, on its solitary way to the great sacrifice of the ages, met for a moment the prudent morality of the good man, and in the flashing of its self-revelation it became as a consuming fire to his hard, dry goodness; but the supreme requirement of that divine Character was never destructive of living joy. Jesus on that same sacrificial journey took little children in his arms and blessed them. Jesus did not ask sacrifices of his disciples because the loss and pain are virtues, but because through them God's will may be carried on to larger good. Let us not wrong the Son of man by putting him into any wrong relation to human life. Asceticism is not sacrifice. St. Francis of Assisi, were he living here and now, might do a nobler work for humanity by setting a good example as a Christian capitalist, upholding other men, building cleanly homes around his factories, and causing his success to bless his city, than he could possibly do by becoming a missionary mendicant. The Christian law of sacrifice has higher claims to-day upon the money-power of the world than could be met by any reckless abandonment of the world's stored up capital. And the law of sacrifice should never be interpreted as a commandment of misery. God does not love wretchedness. Christ in the hour of his full sacrificial consciousness could speak not of his peace only, but also of his joy.

The Lord has put us into this beautiful world not that we may make it a place of torture to us, or so abuse it that our hearts may become places of torment in it. There is a divine blessedness which all life reveals, a joy of the Creator in the light of the morning skies, in the ringing clearness of the winter air, in the laughing of the brooks unchained, in the early spring, in the fresh, abounding life of the summer fields, the colors of each flower, the ever renewed brightness of the earth, and in the happiness of infancy around which "heaven lies." John Calvin, spending most of his theological days in Geneva, in the midst of the joy of that scenery which every traveller delights to remember, though his eye must often have rested upon the blue lake, and the purpling mountains, and before him many an evening the day's afterglow had bloomed upon the distant sky, never, says his biographer, in all his letters makes one allusion to the beauty of the world around him, and God's pleasure in it. Yet in these brief Gospels of the life of Jesus of Nazareth we still love to read of the glory of the lilies, and of the vine and the branches, and the place where there was much grass, and the fisher's boat, and the fields upon which the Saviour glanced, as men love still to look upon a field white for the harvest. A logic which is not open enough to let nature in, is not the logic of the life of the Son of man. A theology of the Cross of Christ which does not make love first and omnipresent, and full always of an eternal joy, is not the truth of God which we may learn from the life and the death of the Son of man. " He shall see of the travail of his soul, and shall be satisfied."

The law of sacrifice, I would declare then, is not a law which puts a premium upon suffering in God's universe, or makes a virtue of unhappiness. It is a law which obtains in a universe made in joy and made for happiness; it is a law of Him who gave his life for the world, and rose again, and sits henceforth expecting upon the throne of God.

Having recognized, thus, that in the divine order sacrifice is the means, and the blessedness of God the end, that the Cross of Christ on earth is for the joy of heaven, and that it was not borne for its own sake, as though God could have pleasure in beholding suffering, we may ask once more, and more discerningly, the question whether every day our lives are held truly under that law of sacrifice, whether when that supreme Character may appear before us in some supreme hour, we shall go away grieved to our possessions, or follow Christ to Jerusalem. This is a question not so much of the quantity of your gifts, though that may help determine it, but of the spirit of your giving. And by giving I do not mean merely giving money. I mean personal giving, often including money, but above all personal giving, like Christ's giving of himself to the world. I mean giving which begins in the heart, and becomes a power of the character, and, working from within as a new birth of the love of God in the soul, sweeps all obstructions of habit and obstacles even of inherited temperament before it, and is the outflow of the life, the influence of the man, filling his whole possible opportunity of good,—even like that virtue of which we read, that it went out from Jesus and healed the suppliant who touched the hem of his garment. How much of that inward sacrificial virtue is there in our characters ready to respond to the slightest touch upon us? How much consecrated personal power is there in our churches, flowing out in all possible ways upon the city, and into this world for which Christ, in the glory of God, went up to Jerusalem to die?

In these days of social seriousness before Easter we may remember him who counted it joy to give his life for the world; we may see the Christ standing even now before this church, as he stood before that good man for a moment, as He was passing on his way to the Cross; and as we grow conscious of his Spirit in us, we may know whether our souls would follow him whatever he would have us do.

Only let us not this morning turn too easily away from that sacred scene of the Gospel. It is no medieval picture. It is a present revelation, and a present judgment. It is here in the Gospel to-day, for the church still to look upon. What willingness of sacrifice for the people has the church of Christ in this country at its heart? The answer to that question is the prophecy of what this land will be at this century's close. To-day there is the scattered home missionary line, skirmishing with the godliness of an eager civilization on the far frontiers, and our Home Missionary society borrowing money to send out necessary supplies! There, opening all around the horizon of Christendom, is the world-opportunity, and the laborers are few; and we believers, alas! are sometimes without faith enough in the Gospel to trust it gladly to any earnest heart that for Christ's dear sake would take it to the perishing. And here at home are the multitudes who hardly know how to live; men discouraged or in temptation who need a kindly, brave word, or a helping hand; and young women, many of them, without homes or good company, working for what pittance they can earn, uneducated, and very likely uninteresting enough except to the God who made them; —and here are Christian girls, refined, and happy, yet without the inspiration of real service in life;— are there not ways, which they by seeking may find, of girding themselves and serving those others, and in serving knowing who Jesus Christ is, and what eternal life is? A religion that costs us nothing is of little value to ourselves or others. Are we spending six days of the week in laying up treasures for ourselves, and then one in praying God to make sure to us our eternal salvation? Master, "Grant unto us that we may sit, one on thy right hand and one on thy left hand, in thy glory." Is discipleship of Christ to become then a crowned selfishness, or must there be some sign of the cross on every crown? "Ye shall indeed drink of the cup that I drink of;"— Jesus knew the disciples, and the power and the task of the grace of God for the disciples, better than they knew themselves and the work in them to be wrought in Christ's name. There is more of the sacrificial spirit of Christ deep down in the heart of our Christianity than sometimes appears. In every crisis, it is true, in every day of the Son of man, there shall be first who shall be last, and last first. That poor unknown saint met duty like a martyr; and that man who was a ruler in Israel flinched in the trial of his manhood. But there always has been, and there is still, the power of the Master's sacrificial spirit among the true disciples. There may indeed be sent times of trial to God's church to bring that spirit out. The wisest cannot tell what destructive forces are gathering beneath the surface of our industrial civilization. One heroic age of our country has become a memory, and one of the last and most eminent of the patriots and lovers of liberty whose soul was fashioned, and tempered, and set aflame by it, has just passed beyond our praises or our blame.* Sometimes one could almost pray that providence might kindle again flaming questions of liberty and humanity, if only to bring out men, and to show once more the possibilities of sacrifice in women.

But now there are rung out no sudden alarms, and no great appeals of duty command us all; yet there is a work to be accomplished for Christ and our

* Henry Ward Beecher.

country, before which earnest souls should feel straitened until it be done; and we need for its vast achievement that spirit in all our churches which He required who said to the young ruler, "Come, take up the cross, and follow me." No community can be saved without sacrifice. Somebody's sacrifice is in every blessing we have received. No church can be great without sacrifice. No home can be blessed without the sacrificial spirit. No soul can become fit for the kingdom of heaven without the consecration of the Spirit.

We cannot put off the supreme requirement of that supreme Character which confronts us with its commandment of divine perfection, by contenting ourselves with any partial response to it. When Jesus on the way to Jerusalem asked that youth to give up his possessions, what think you that the Lord cared for that man's money? He did not need a shekel of it. Judas might have asked a higher price for his treachery if he had had more in the bag. The disciples did not need that ruler's property. They were better off without it. That fine example of charity in the first church at Jerusalem might have been lost from Christian history, if that ruler's possessions had been given and invested in real estate for the Christians at Jerusalem. It was not the ruler's money that Jesus cared for when he bade him sell all, and give to the poor. He wanted the man. And he could not get the man unless he saved him from his money. Jesus wanted that man's will of life. He wanted that man's whole purpose. He wanted that man's heart. Money enough will go to the Lord's exchangers, if the church can put heart enough into the Lord's service. Where your heart is, there will your money be found also. And what humanity all around us needs is first and above all the heart of the church, freely, joyously given in Christ's name to Christ's service.

XV.

MISUNDERSTANDING CHRIST.

"And they understood none of these things; and this saying was hid from them, and they perceived not the things that were said."—LUKE xviii. 34.

THIS verse of Luke's Gospel records the disciples' acknowledgment that at the time Jesus was going up to Jerusalem to be crucified they had not understood him. Luke takes pains to put into his narrative three distinct avowals that the disciples had misunderstood Jesus' words. "And they understood none of these things; and this saying was hid from them, and they perceived not the things that were said."

No living men had known Jesus so well as those disciples had known him. They had been his nearest friends. They had been some three years with Jesus in his daily ministry. Yet the Christ must go to the hour of his trial in utter solitude of spirit, every hosanna of the people a misunderstanding of his sacrificial will, and not a thought of his chosen friends reaching into the deeper purpose of his obedience unto death.

The disciples' failure to understand the Master suggests an always timely question for the followers of Jesus: What misunderstandings of Christ may still be lingering in Christianity? Is it possible that we may as strangely misunderstand our Master and Lord?

The question is the more pertinent and the more

necessary because one reason for the disciples' failure to perceive the things that were said by Jesus on his way to the Cross, was the knowledge of him which they already possessed. Because already they partly understood him, and his Messianic mission, this other saying in its fuller revelation of the Christ was hid from them. They already understood him in some respects so well, that they were not ready or willing to receive a revelation which went beyond their thought of him. Their partial understanding of him, in their contentment in it, became an obstacle to a complete knowledge of him. The truth which they had already learned of him they could fit for the most part into their previous habits of thought concerning the Messiah, and it satisfied their ideas of what his kingdom on earth should be; so that when Jesus would begin with their partial understanding of him, and proceed to lead them out into a larger and diviner knowledge of God's will, they were not able to break loose from their comfortable contentment in the truth which they already had received. Hence while these disciples cherish in their hearts the thought that the Messiah is already in the way which leads up to his kingdom, and their thrones, the Christ goes before them, alone in the Spirit, knowing that the Cross is first God's will, and then the coming of the kingdom of heaven.

There may have been some willfulness in the disciples' failure to understand new truth from Jesus; very likely there was resistance of habit, and obstinacy of desire, such as we may often observe in the way of men's larger knowledge of truth; but it is clear also that the disciples stopped short, well satisfied with some truths which they had already learned of Jesus, and thus were prevented from going on with Christ in his further revelation of God's will.

Two truths in particular which they had learned better than any one else concerning Jesus, they allowed to stand in the way of their further understanding of him. They had been taught his wonderful power. They had been eye-witnesses of his mighty works. They knew, as others had not had so good opportunities of knowing, that Jesus' miracles were not carefully prepared deceptions, or results of some studied mastery of occult arts. They knew that his miracles were spontaneous, and natural to the Christ. They were the immediate outgoings of the power of the Man. He himself was the cause of which his works of healing were the effects. Virtue went out from him. He was always greater than his works. The Man was more than all that he did. That they had seen and learned. They began to believe that Jesus could do anything. This truth of the power of the Son of man they were ready to receive, and they stopped with the knowledge of it. He who had power from God could not be taken and killed by the Pharisees. So they grasped with eager hope the truth that Jesus was the promised Messiah of Israel, and missed the deeper truth of his character, that God so loved the world.

Then again the truth which they had learned better than any others of Jesus' wonderful kindness, and justice, and humanity, in their partial view of it, may have hidden from their eyes the full revelation which he would have them perceive of his divine life. How could he who had power over death, and who had so pitied two sisters that he had restored their brother to them, and who had enveloped their lives in a friendship of wonderful daily thoughtfulness,—how could he, having all power, go away from them, leave them comfortless, throw them back again upon the world, and disappoint their high hopes of him? No wonder Peter thought it was impossible, and even said impulsively, "Be it far from thee, Lord!" The truth of Christ's friendship which they did know prevented them from understanding the diviner secret of God's sacrificial love for the world, which they might have learned. So they who knew the Lord best, misunderstood him the most; and Jesus went before his disciples in a deeper purpose and a diviner thought than they perceived.

You see thus how closely the question may always come home to Christians concerning their understanding, and misunderstandings, of Christ and his kingdom. And a brief glance at the history of Christ's revelation of the Father since those early days will serve to give to the question still more pertinency and point. For the history of Christ's church in this world has been one repeated process of partial understandings of Christ, with misunderstandings, and then new and larger understandings of his words. Men have learned some truth of Christ, and gone bravely off with it, and embodied it in the institutions of Christianity, or put it into their creeds, and stopped contented with that lesson of the Christ as though they understood him perfectly. And then that partial idea of what the Gospel is, or the church should be, has proved a barrier to progress, and the stream has been checked, and the scum of many corruptions has gathered on its surface, until some refreshing from on high has swept again all barriers away. At first perhaps the new flood seemed to be a destructive torrent, but at length the purified stream. and more fruitful fields on either side, have proved that it was a new inflowing of power from on high.

The history of the Christian church discovers this threefold process often repeated,—first some true, but partial lesson learned of Jesus Christ; then the Church's contentment with that lesson, and teaching the people to repeat it by rote; and then some providential task and trial, and under the necessity of an age the discovery of some new meaning in the old truths, or some fresh interpretation of the words of God which at first disciples had not understood, and a new Christian movement, a reformation, a greater work of faith, another of the days of the Son of man.

It is always in order, therefore, for us to ask, Are we stopping short with lessons of Christ already learned? Are we in aught misunderstanding Christianity?

In order that we may bring this matter more closely home to ourselves some further preliminary remarks should be made. Our text reads like a devout apology of the disciples for their singular misunderstanding of Jesus Christ. The providence of God had taught them their mistake. And very instructive for us is the method by which God corrected the false perception of the disciples, and opened their eyes to true and larger knowledge of the Lord. They overcame their misunderstanding, and were brought to better understanding of Jesus Christ, through the trial and the task of their faith. These two, trials and tasks, are God's ways of correcting men's imperfect faiths. For you will recall how those disciples, at the time of the crucifixion, and while they were waiting in Jerusalem, learned in their disenchantment, and were taught through that fearful strain and trial of their faith, as they had never seen before, of what spirit Jesus was, and what his real mission to this world was; and thus they were prepared to see and to become apostles of the risen Lord. That trial of their faith, while Jesus was mocked, and scourged, and delivered to death, and crucified between two thieves, and buried,—all the light blotted from their skies, all the proud ambition broken in their souls,—yet in his death a new, strange expectancy awakened in their hearts, and on the third day a vision seen which made all things a new world to them,—that trial of their faith was the Lord's method of teaching the disciples what before had remained hidden from them even in plainest words of Jesus. And then this knowledge of the new, larger truth of Christ's work was rounded out, and filled full of a steady, clear light to them, by the task immediately given them to do in the name of the crucified and risen Lord. They learned at Pentecost what Christianity was to be. Peter learned it still further when a trial of his faith came to him in a vision on the house-top, and while he doubted what it meant, a work from God was given him by the messengers at the door. St. Paul learned to know Christ after the Spirit with an ever progressive knowledge through the trials and the tasks of his ministry. And I might continue with many an historical illustration to show how the providence of God, at sundry times, has corrected inherited or congenial misunderstandings of Christianity, and given to each notable Christian age its new theology by means of the trials and the tasks of its faith. Interesting, however, as such historical illustrations of God's methods are, let us seek rather to bring these general truths as quickly as possible to a focus upon ourselves. By our trial and our task of faith God's providence may be clearing up some of our misunderstandings of the Lord's words.

Our trial of faith comes to us mainly from the intellectual side. It is witnessed by the difficulty which many of you men feel in forming strong convictions on any religious subject. Ours is not a trial of faith by persecutions or martyrdoms. Occasionally we may be made to stumble over some hard piece of medievalism which has been left in the way; but usually that proves to be only an irritation rather than a trial of our faith; and in these days, even from a worldly point of view, it is no loss to a man to join a Christian church. The world has become in its manners and social usages so far Christianized that there is very little outwardly which he may be called upon to give up. It may cost him something to help support the Christian religion; but not nearly so much as the heathen often pay in the worship of their idols. Protestant Christianity seems to be the least expensive of the religions of the world, notwithstanding its frequent contribution-boxes, and foreign missions!

Yet in our time we have had trial enough of faith from the intellectual side. Indeed, there are so many things now to be thought of, that religion, although acknowledged to be the chief concern, seems to be crowded out of the lives of many intellectual men. Religious questions, they think, can wait; other problems of thought and life are pressing. One peculiar trial of our faith arises from the dissipation of convictions among multitudinous things, newly discovered, partly known, everywhere rising up to interest us, and presenting to our reasons questions not lightly to be put aside. And the effect of this peculiar trial of faith is a certain faintheartedness among believers, or half-belief, or make-believe, or even a cowardly falling back and huddling together of frightened believers, like an army in a panic, upon old intrenchments from which they had marched out with banners flying. Such briefly is our trial of faith; but put beside it, as God's providence does actually bind up with it, our task of faith. It is easy to see what that is. Is it not the great missionary work? I use the word in its truest and broadest sense. Our task is the work of the missionary church. Our Christianity is nothing save as it is a missionary Christianity. It is to be a witness of Christ "both in Jerusalem,"—and that means for us in the center of our own city, —"and in all Judea,"—that means for us all New England,—"and in Samaria,"—and that means in the Indian reservations, and on the far frontiers of American civilization,—"and unto the uttermost part of the earth." I need not delay to argue the matter; for what observant Christians do not perceive that the task which is laid with urgent necessity upon our common Christianity, is to establish the kingdom of God here on this earth, in human society, and to make the whole world Christian? A most singular providential coincidence surely, and very instructive for us,—this subtle intellectual trial of faith, and this great task of world-wide missions, laid in one and the same hour upon the Church of God.

This twofold providence is bringing out for all who have eyes to see, a fresh interpretation of what Christianity is. And as we catch some glimpse of it, we find it inspiring and grand. We behold once more a lifting up of Christ himself before the world to draw all men unto him. We are going back to where the first disciples began their knowledge of the Christian life, even to Christ himself, to his character, his life and death, his personal revelation of God and the will of God. In that hour when the disciples began to understand his words which had been hidden from them, when on that first day of the week they were gathered together, we read that Jesus himself stood in the midst of them. That scene is the frontispiece of Christian history. Jesus himself in the midst of his disciples;—that is Christianity. Christianity, true, living Christianity, is not the Bible of the Protestants, not the Church of the Roman Catholics, not the creeds of the ecumenical councils. Christianity *has* a creed, but it is more than a creed; it *has* a Bible, but it is more than the Bible; Christianity is Jesus himself in the midst of men; it is the Spirit of Christ in the life of humanity. Our trial and our task of faith are combining to throw all churches back directly upon the Christ of the Gospels. Let biblical or historical criticism tear away from Christian beliefs anything that may prove to be adventitious, traditional, or unverifiable; let an eager science press open door within door of this mysterious succession of things which we call nature; suffer honest thought to penetrate as far as it may into the secrets of life, and the creation's history;— at the beginning is a Power which we cannot compass, and at the end a Purpose which we cannot measure, and at the center, in the focus of all our earthly lights, a Character having the glory of God, which we cannot question. That Character is the ultimate of our moral knowledge. It is center and source of life in a new moral creation. It is revelation of God. It is motive-power of a world's salvation. Doubt, brought at last before that ultimate and commanding Character, meets the transcendent affirmation of God in the life of humanity. Christ is the "I am" of God confronting here upon this earth all our human denials. "Before Abraham was, I am;"—Eternal righteousness and truth, Eternal Love dwells among men incarnate, and its Gospel never to be silenced, is, "I am;" "Verily, verily, I say unto you;" "Believe me."

Thus the trial of our faith presses us back to Christ himself; and no less the task of faith compels us to preach Christ, and constrains us, like the Apostle of the Gentiles, not to know any thing among men save Christ Jesus and him crucified.

Observe how this providential return of Christianity to Christ himself in the midst of his disciples is correcting misunderstandings of him, is leading the general Christian consciousness to seize with a new enthusiasm upon the vital, essential truths of the Gospel which meet the real wants of real life, and how, on account of our searching trial and our mighty task of faith, we are learning to pour contempt upon one after another of our hindering, and divisive, and paralyzing misunderstandings of what pure Christianity should be. The Church would loiter far behind the providence of God in the missionary call of our century, should it linger and lag, overweighted, under the burdens of the inherited mistakes or dogmatisms of good men who have not always appreciated the simplicity of the Gospel, nor its universality. Jesus himself in the midst of his disciples, the Spirit of Christ in the midst of consecrated men and women,—oh! this is not what a church has sometimes misconceived itself to be. This real Church of Christ is not a band of thinkers bound together by a confession of formal propositions mostly true; nor is it a mystical body having its heart in a sacrament; nor an elect company waiting for thrones; nor a favored society, sufficient unto itself, a special assembly whose names are written on pew doors! Not such is the conception of the Church which we see when we look back and behold Jesus himself, in the midst of his disciples, going about doing good, now on the streets of Capernaum, healing the sick, now among the lepers and those possessed with devils, now in the temple driving out the money-changers, or teaching the scribes a divinity simple and sincere as the love of God, and human as the joy of the Father over the prodigal who was lost and is found. Jesus himself, the serene, radiant, helpful One, doing God's will, Jesus himself, the risen, adorable Master and Lord in the midst of his disciples whom he sends forth in his Spirit as his apostles, —oh, that is the true Church, the Church against which the gates of the hell of the city's lusts and sins shall not prevail, the Church to which all power is given! Something like this, something more like this than we, or our fathers, have seen, is the Church of God for which men are looking, blindly, ignorantly ofttimes it may be, but after which the world is seeking as its social Messiah, for the salvation of the lives and the homes of the people in all these manufacturing towns and villages of New England, and in every land, and now especially in India and Japan. In the name of the Son of man let us be ashamed of, and at any cost to our habits or our pride let us repent of, any ideas of the Christianity of Jesus Christ which we may have shared, which have been less broad, less sympathetic, less divinely human, than this vision of Jesus himself in the midst of his disciples in the world.

And I want to leave this sermon resting in its more personal applications. We ought to search our conduct of life and our habits of thought to learn whether personally and privately we are still misunderstanding the Lord's word to us, when we may come to a better understanding of it. Are we being *mastered* by the character of the Lord Jesus Christ? That is the real question of personal religion. What does that mastery of a man involve? Anything more than I am now doing, or giving of myself? Anything other than I have been doing for years, and years, and years? Some of you, who have long heard Christ preached, have not many years more at the longest to live in this world,—five, ten, twenty years perhaps longer, if no accident overtakes you, and you are permitted to fill out the full circle of the life allotted to man. Is there anything left that you have not yet brought under the mastery of the Lord Jesus Christ? Do you own anything over which you cannot write in good conscience, Christ is Lord? Can you with sincere judgment subscribe beneath every paragraph and codicil of your life's will and testament, as you pray here in this church, " For the sake of Jesus Christ, Amen?" Because our whole will and testament of life shall be probated not on earth merely, but by the Lord who has given to every man his talent, and also these opportunities of good in which any talent may be put to his exchangers and multiplied.

To us all, old and young, the duty comes this day once more of judging for ourselves, and deciding, whether we have been misunderstanding, whether we are willing to understand, the word of God to us personally through the life and death of Jesus Christ. Lord what would'st thou have me do? I own thy divine mastery; what would'st thou have me do? I am as nothing; but I will do it. By thy grace, Lo, I come to do thy will, O God.

XVI.

PUTTING THE WITNESS AWAY.

"But the chief priests took counsel that they might put Lazarus also to death; because that by reason of him many of the Jews went away, and believed on Jesus."—JOHN xii. 10–11.

FOR the past few Sundays I have taken my texts from those scenes in the life of Christ which the Evangelists represent as having occurred at this period of the year between the closing days of February and the early part of April. During these weeks the Son of man dwelt in the certain and near prospect of his Cross. His words and his character at this time evidently made a supreme impression upon the disciples,—the Gospel narratives grow full and clear at this epoch of our Lord's life; and if we have eyes to see the wonderful sacrificial Character which then began more fully to disclose its divine purpose and power to the disciples, and which afterwards they understood, we shall find our lives brought under a commanding influence, superior to all other motives which may attract us. Let a man once really see and feel these two things,—the humanity which he shares with all others, and the salvation of that humanity in the Person of Jesus Christ, which he with all men may possess;—let a man once really know these two things, the sinful, anxious, loveless humanity which is lost in the world, and the rich, full, and redeemed humanity which is found in the Person of Jesus Christ in the midst of his disciples,—

and the clear perception of these two opposite things, contrasted as death and life, will henceforth hold that man under the power of a new motive, and pervade his whole soul with a consecration and enthusiasm for the kingdom of God's sake.

The narratives of the Gospels which depict the closing scenes of Jesus' life bring out the most marked and startling contrasts. We see Jesus on his way to the Cross, drawing near to Bethany; and within the walls of Jerusalem we look upon another scene in the tragedy of the sin of the world, and observe what the chief priests and rulers of the Jews were doing, in the hour of Christ, when he was approaching Jerusalem. Beyond the holy city, in the quietness of Ephraim, Jesus has been revealing God to willing, but misunderstanding disciples; and already on the way up to Jerusalem he begins to show himself openly to the people. Within the city of the prophets those Jews have been taking counsel, and plotting together; blinding each other, and strengthening one another in hatred and pride, they have been preparing to enact, hardly knowing what they did, the great crime of history.

The conduct of those men in Jerusalem presents the chief difficulty in the way of the hope which all Christlike hearts would cherish of some final universal salvation. For those Jews in Jerusalem, hardening themselves against Christ, reveal the power of the human heart to grow malignant, and to become utterly blinded to truth, even while the Life of Love is an increasing light of God's presence round about it. That council of desperate rulers which was held while Jesus was on his way to Jerusalem, shows how obdurate the human will may grow when divinity draws near its gates, and the Christ could weep over its destruction. The thought that checks and chills the natural Christian hope that all souls at last may be restored, does not arise while we are walking with Jesus on his way to the city. He has come to seek the lost. Salvation can hardly depend upon one's happening to be sitting by the way-side when Jesus of Nazareth is passing by. He who came to seek the lost,—shall he not in his own times, and to the utmost power of his love, seek up and down all the ways of his creation for those who are lost? But the difficulty is that those Jews in Jerusalem, having eyes, see not; and though none of the people are more darkly lost than they, they will not be found. "And ye would not!" was Jesus' lamentation over the city of the prophets. The mercy of the Lord—so Israel was assured even in the Old Testament, when revelation was not yet far from Sinai—is a mercy which endureth forever, a mercy from everlasting to everlasting. We may easily believe that the Love which by its nature is eternal cannot subject itself in its divine seeking to limits of time or place. The difficulty in the hope of universal salvation is not to be found in the nature of God, not at the Cross of Christ, not in any temporal bounds put upon the omnipresence of the Spirit of Christ; but the obstacle, at which our knowledge must stop, lies deep in the will of man, and its fearful possibilities of evil. We recall how those Jews at the very hour of the revelation of the most adorable Character upon which human eyes had ever looked, blinded themselves to its glory, mocked and rejected it, crucified Love, and would nail Truth itself to a cross. That tragic scene, and all repetitions of that fearful exhibition of the power of sin, do not permit us to accept as an induction from human experience the dogma of a universal salvation; as, on the other hand, a simple deduction from the Christlikeness of God's nature, as that is revealed in the New Testament, leaves us no reason to doubt, or to deny, that God in Christ to the utmost extent of moral possibility will be his own missionary, the first and the last, to all souls of men;—our missionary service is but our part and privilege in the divine work of the redemption of the world. Exactly what shall become of Caiaphas and those Sadducees, and of Judas too, when Christ's kingdom shall have reached its completion, his judgment come, and God will be all in all, these Gospels do not undertake to declare; and he who would presume to preach in this matter the whole counsel of God is in danger of being bold beyond what is written, or can be known by us in our present schoolterm of existence. That man may need to be warned against the mistake of the scribes who would put upon our ancient and apostolic Christianity any burden of his private interpretation too great for it to bear. Meanwhile, this one revelation is plainly to be seen,—and it were harmful sentiment to turn our eyes altogether from it, for human history shows and repeats in a thousand scenes this one tragic spectacle,—Jesus Christ in the sacrificial power of love drawing near the city, and men within, even in mercy's hour, preparing to crucify him.

From the description of what was passing in the

minds of those men in Jerusalem, I have taken for our special lesson this morning a text which discloses an incidental and subsidiary thought which they entertained. "They sought to put Lazarus also to death." We are so bound together in one common humanity that we can enter into the consciousness of the best and the worst of men, and understand both the great virtues and the great crimes of history. We hear the story of some magnificent deed and we can feel burning within us the high resolves which made that heroism possible; our thought can interpret another's noble deed. And the skillful lawyer, pleading in our courts, knowing the common motives and the common experiences of men, will unravel the skein of circumstances which bound the criminal in a net-work of temptations, deceptions, and evil deeds; and a jury of twelve ordinary men, from their common knowledge of human passions can judge whether the crime were possible or not, as another man stands charged with it. We are all of us sinful enough to comprehend the sin of the world. On the one hand we have instincts of the true, we have intimations of the Spirit within us, pure enough, and noble, to enable us to follow the Son of man who is in the way going up to Jerusalem; and also we are sinners enough to enter into the counsels of the Jews within the city.

It is not difficult for us to understand the simple reason given in the narrative why they would put Lazarus also to death. "Because that by reason of him many of the Jews went away, and believed on Jesus."

That thought of those priests, that desperate

thought, was only an exaggeration of a common tendency of our human nature. That counsel of the chief priests presents in a magnified form a natural disposition which lies in a diminutive and undeveloped state, but capable under temptation of great possibility of evil, in the minds of all of us. As we are capable of it, and in what may seem unimportant habits may have yielded to it, it lies within us, one of the evil dispositions of human nature, one of the possibilities of sin and death, which we have inherited, and from which we should seek to become free.

For consider how natural that counsel of those Jews was. They had no special spite against Lazarus himself. He was a quiet man apparently, who had lived a quiet life out under the olive-trees at Bethany. But they did not wish Christ to take their power from them, and although as consistent Sadducees they could not allow themselves to believe in the resurrection, the continued existence of Lazarus was an unwelcome suggestion to them of its possibility, and an evidence of it which was misleading the people. They would not receive any proof of the resurrection, nor tolerate Jesus, preaching the Gospel of it. Dogmatists always must close their minds against evidences of new truth. Naturally they seek to put the witness to it out of the way. Of old they thought of killing Lazarus. Fifteen hundred years later the same men would have thought of putting him to the rack, and torturing him until he recanted. Eighteen hundred years later they would have thought only of breaking down his influence by misrepresentation and appeals to popular prejudice in the newspaper organs of their sect. The world moves, and Christ's Spirit grows in the thoughts of men's hearts, and the same evil disposition which of old would have put Lazarus to death assumes in our counsels and conversation milder and more polite, but perhaps hardly less sinful forms. If we do not want to receive Christ, or some truth of his revealing, the next and natural thing for us to do is to put out of the way anything that may remind us of it. We have done something like that in lesser things a thousand times. Some truth we had made up our minds we would not listen to, and we put its Lazarus out of the way. Some word of the Lord drew near us, and was about to revolutionize our life for us, and we did not want to see our world changed, and we thought how we might silence its chosen witness.

I might draw many an illustration of this common desire of human nature to put Lazarus out of the way, from the counsels of men's hearts in other than religious matters. Do you not remember, some of you? those troubled days before the war, when the storm portent was already visible in our Southern skies, and the cloud was growing, and there were men in our Northern cities who would not see it, merchants who did not wish to have their commerce interfered with and their profits stopped, timid and selfish politicians who for the sake of office, and their ease, were willing to reject the truth of freedom and the redeemed nation which was already on its way through suffering towards its kingdom and its crown; and because those men would not be its disciples, ready to give up all for it, they sought also to put down every Lazarus whose presence was leading the people away after that new faith; and even when its hour was at hand, they said, "It cannot be; this Truth shall not reign over us; we will not let it come and take the peace of compromise away from our nation: we have no king but Cotton! Let us hustle down from the platforms, and put out of our pulpits all men who are witnesses of the higher law, for the people are going away after them!" Truly it is human nature, and we all share it, to put Lazarus also to death.

I might open the book of the lives of the witnesses and martyrs in the generations past, and find on many a page illustration of this our inherited and common tendency of evil which leads men's thoughts to take counsel against Lazarus; as Roman emperors, when they would stop the growth of the new religion, became persecutors of Christianity, and as Julian the Apostate with a more crafty tolerance sought to suppress Christianity by prohibiting Christian schools; or as the papacy, in its effort to suppress the better spirit stirring in its midst, sent Savonarola to the stake; as priestcraft would have shattered the telescope in which the heavens began to reveal their glory; and as even to this day we sometimes imagine we can prevent wild social movements which threaten our vested rights, by sturdily refusing to inquire what unheeded truths may possibly lie beneath them, or what more human Gospel may be waiting to enter all our cities. But it is never candid, or quite honest, to think of putting Lazarus also to death.

I wish, however, to trace this common tendency

in our minds through some of its religious processes.

An obvious and gross exemplification of it is the counsel of irreligious men to put the Church, or the Bible, out of the way. Religion cannot be thrown off by the people while these witnesses remain. Therefore ridicule the Bible, and attack the Church. And in this matter the instinct of irreligion is not on a false scent. The social Sadducees cannot secure their reign in an anarchical humanity, so long as the people have the Bible in their homes, with its Hebrew teaching of the sovereignty of God's law, and so long as the churches stand to bear witness to the Gospel of Christ. The Christian Church is to the successive generations what Lazarus was to those common people who came, " not for Jesus' sake only, but that they might see Lazarus also, whom he had raised from the dead." For the Christian Church, so far as it breathes the Master's spirit, is as one raised from the dead to newness of life. It exists as the continual proof and witness among men of the divine Power which has rolled away the stone from the sepulchre of man's death in sin, and said with a loud voice, " Come forth." The napkin indeed may be still bound over the face of the witness to Christ's power, and the smell of the corruptions of the world still be about the garments of the Church; but, dumb and scarce saved from the power of evil though it may sometimes seem to be, it is living, and it witnesses to a new life of humanity; it proclaims by its mere presence here the redeeming grace of God. As it takes up again familiar duties in a grateful love, and looks out to behold a fresh light and a new sanctity upon this old earth, and abides at the hearth of humanity in a love possessed now of an assured consciousness of immortality, the Church of Christ, living, redeemed, sanctified, is the true witness to the Christ from God. Atheism, anarchism, the powers of darkness, must put this Lazarus to death, or the people will go away, and believe on Jesus.

There was one thing which those Jews in Jerusalem seem not to have taken sufficiently into their counsels against Lazarus also. Even had they succeeded in ridding themselves of Lazarus' uncomfortable presence, they would still have been compelled to confront in their temple Jesus himself. He did at length meet them on their own ground. He went to Jerusalem. He taught in the temple. He stood before the Sanhedrim. "Behold, the Man!" Behold those chief priests and rulers. "I judge no man," said Jesus. "And yet if I judge, my judgment is true."

Our witness to Christ we grant is imperfect. Lazarus may not always have borne in mind through what a mighty change he had passed. The old ways come back, and the new life may seem at times like a dream. But, nevertheless, there is renewed Christian character enough in any common church, always present, to bear witness to the Christ who has raised it from its death of sin. It is not altogether candid, nor honest, to let that present and living proof of Christ be to a man's reason as though it were not.

Let us trace this evil tendency of our thoughts still nearer and closer. There are hours when the Christ

Putting the Witness Away. 207

draws nigh the cities of our souls. There are personal approaches and appeals of the Lord to our characters. For the religion which we profess, and to which the Church is called to testify by its experience of redemption, is not a merely intellectual creed, nor emotional state; it is a creed of character; it is a state of life. And Christ has many and various forms of appearing among the disciples, the same true Master and Lord in all. Christ may come near us from God in a duty, in some privilege, in an opportunity, in a clearer perception of truth. How do we receive these approaches of our Lord? What counsel do our thoughts take concerning the things which may remind us of him? There was a duty drawing nigh in the name of the Lord; we saw it would interfere with our plan of life. It might disturb our ease; it might spoil our pleasure; it might break our dream of power; it might leave us even out of place, or poorer in pocket. We began to be afraid that our thoughts would so go out towards it, and dwell upon it, that some day we should find that duty in the name of Christ reigning over us. And there was something near at hand which reminded us of it. At least we could get rid of that. It may have been the sight of a friend. We avoided that friend. It may have been some spectacle of want or suffering. We passed by on the other side. It may have been some inward feeling, some thought, which, whenever it came to us, recalled that duty, suggested that sacrifice, was a witness to that one thing which we ought to do. And we took pains to avoid those feelings or thoughts; we hurried from anything that might bring them before us. So we remembered to forget that duty. We put its Lazarus where he would not trouble us.

Christ draws near souls sometimes in some new, almost strange sense of faith, or hope, or possibility of life richer, and truer, and happier. It is with us as though a door were for a moment flung open into some lovelier world, and radiant spirits strong and full of life passed before us, and we see what better days might be for us also, and then we turn, and other desires of life gather quickly around us, and " the vision splendid " fades " into the light of common day." We belong to the world again; we throw ourselves with fresh abandonment into it; we enjoy its frolic, and are for the most part happy and careless enough; but the memory of that door, once flung open into something truer, and diviner, dwells still within us. That vision keeps coming back to us, our soul's witness to Christ. Will we put that witness also to death?

In those days of old, when Christ came to Bethany, Lazarus was a proof of immortality to all who saw him. His presence on earth testified to a power which is not of this earth. The evidence of eternal life is always present, stronger than death, in our perpetual human sense of God, in our witness of conscience, in the instinct which cannot be silenced of human love. Little account indeed may this witness of God in us be able to give of itself as we question it; little memory may it have of its hour of awakening in the soul of man; but it is here with us, and in the life of humanity, even as Lazarus was in the home of Bethany, the living witness of the word of Jesus Christ. We have this real, vital, consciousness of God and hope of immortality present with man to this day, God's proof, and God's power in the thought and the heart of humanity. It were not candid, it is not honest, to ignore it, or to plot how we can put this witness of God to death in the thoughts of our hearts. Let us cherish and honor it, and keep it at its true worth, as the witness and pledge of the Divine Power which is around us, and which is always repeating its miracle by bidding true life come forth from the dead.

Question, study, investigate, doubt, inquire, reason, as the mind must or may; Jesus Christ never forbade any man to ask his question of him;—but let us be careful,—as we would not reject God himself, and blind ourselves to his revelation,—let us be careful, how we turn from, or neglect, or wish to put out of the way any presence, or word, or duty, which witnesses of Diviner things than we know, and which may prove to be to our experience of the world as that man was to the disciples the witness by whom Christ's power has been confirmed.

Let me leave the lesson of the text with any to whom Christ is drawing very nigh, and who really intend some day to crown him in their lives. Do not seek to put out of mind those thoughts, those suggestions, and those remembered words, or those witnesses of your own experience, by which often you have been almost persuaded to let yourselves be Christians.

XVII.

A STUDY FOR A DOCTRINE OF THE ATONEMENT.

"Behold, we go up to Jerusalem; and the Son of man shall be delivered unto the chief priests and scribes; and they shall condemn him to death, and shall deliver him unto the Gentiles to mock, and to scourge, and to crucify: and the third day he shall be raised up."—MATT. xx. 18–19.

THESE Scriptures disclose Jesus' final consciousness of the necessity of his sufferings. He knew that his life was to be finished under the law of suffering for sin. The cup could not pass from him.

That law of suffering for sin under which he must bow in his sinless majesty, as though he himself were worthy of death, was no outward necessity, or compulsion of physical force. The miracle-worker could have saved himself from those poor, cowardly Jews in Jerusalem. No hostile power led the Lord as a captive in the way up to Jerusalem. Jesus knew that at his command legions of angels were waiting. Having all power, he submitted himself to some universal moral law of suffering for sin. The doctrine of the atonement is an attempt on the part of believers to comprehend that higher law of suffering in the forgiveness of sin. The Gospels declare the fact of Christ's death for us, and disclose Jesus' clear and certain consciousness that his sufferings were necessary for the completion of his work.

But the New Testament dwells mainly upon the fact that Christ must needs suffer, and affords only passing glimpses into the reasons in God's mind for Christ's death. To accept the simple fact, and to build all our hopes upon it, is the chief concern of our Christian faith. Yet the Gospel is a gift of God to the human reason, as well as to the human heart, and consequently the Church has always pondered over the deep necessities in the holy love of God for the atoning sufferings of our Lord.

In other than religious matters we are not content to rest in the simple facts which may present themselves to our observation, but we seek constantly to bring all the facts of our experience into relation and order, or to find the place of each separate thing under some one general law of being. This is the scientific habit of mind, and it is the strongest mental habit of our age. Theology, therefore, as it would fall in with this resistless tendency of men's minds, will seek to bring the moral, spiritual, and divine elements of human life and history under some conception of law, and to view, especially, all the Christian facts as events in one divine order of the universe. Biblical faiths which, taken singly, might seem incredible become reasonable faiths when they are seen to constitute one consistent and harmonious order and law of revelation. I must believe that in answer to the prayer of reason for light, and in reward for modern scientific fidelity, God is discovering to our Christian theology conceptions of the supreme facts of our religion in which they still command rational consent. We are learning to see that the supernatural is most natural; and to read creation and history as one revelation and Gospel of divine truth and love. I think profound reasons may be won from the depths of modern scepticism for new faith in the Incarnation, the miracles, the atoning death, and the resurrection of Jesus Christ, as these events are regarded as constituting one divine order and disclosing one law of love. In the growing conviction that all the Christian faiths are in profoundest accordance with ultimate law, I wish to bring to your thoughts this morning a study for the doctrine of the atonement. I call it only a study for a doctrine, because no creed contains a complete doctrine of Christ's atoning sacrifice. And one reason why churches have been divided, and theology itself brought into contempt in the world, is because men have gone off satisfied with their studies of God's truth as though these were the truth itself, the whole truth, and nothing but the truth.

The explanations which believers in other times have sought to give of the reasons why Christ must needs suffer, have been efforts on their part to bring the fact of Christ's death into some intelligible relation to their prevalent ideas, and general habits of mind. It is a very interesting study to trace the connection between the theology of the Church concerning Christ's work, and the leading ideas, or current philosophies of different times. In this manner, by the effort of each age to interpret Christ and Christianity to itself, all our traditional theories, or doctrines of the nature of the atonement have been formed. The early Christian fathers, for instance, lived in a world which in accordance with much traditional philosophy of their age they were predisposed to look upon as a world belonging to Satan, and justly forfeited to him by sin. Naturally, therefore, in accordance with the prevalent thought of their day, they regarded the death of Christ as a ransom which Jesus paid for sinners to the Evil One. Christ went down to death for man, but the devil, outwitted by the wisdom which he had sought to deceive, could not hold within his power the divine Hostage after he had let the captives for his sake go free. We may smile at this primitive and crude attempt to understand why Christ must needs suffer, but we may profitably remember that to the ancient fathers it was an endeavor to bring the fact of Christ's death into harmony with their thought of the world, and precisely that every Christian generation, which would be honest with itself, will seek to do. This primitive conception of Christ's death as a ransom paid to the devil, lost something of its crudeness in the more spiritualized thought of the later fathers who still held it; and from the first it represented a genuine experience, in the early Church, of redemption by the power of Christ from the evil of the world.

Several centuries later Anselm thought out his masterly conception of the satisfaction of God through the atonement of the Godman. Again in a great thinker's mind the Cross of Christ was set in the midst of the thought of an age. For Anselm's theory of satisfaction is thoroughly Germanic in its origin, and can be understood only as we familiarize ourselves with the Germanic ideas of the reparation which may be made for an offense to the person who has been injured. Either some personal satisfaction through some recompense worthy the honor of the person injured, and adequate to the offense committed, must be rendered, or punishment must be inflicted. The satisfaction was not thought of as some legal equivalent of the punishment of the law, but to the Germanic sense of right either some fitting satisfaction or punishment was the rule of honor.* The sense of personal right, and of what may be due in honor to it, pervades Anselm's thought of the satisfaction which Christ by his act of atoning suffering has rendered to the honor of God. So chivalry passed by, and gave its interpretation of the Cross.

Still later the conceptions of the atonement, variously modified, which we have inherited through Calvinism, were largely drawn from, and corresponded to, juridical and governmental ideas which belong to Roman jurisprudence and the common law. The conception, for example, of Christ's death as the payment of a debt by substitution, is in accordance with the old common law principle that any debt, however large, may be redeemed by any thing offered, and received, as an accepted substitute for its redemption.

To many thoughtful minds, however, these traditional conceptions of the atonement have grown to be distant, and unreal; they sound to them like far-off murmurs of receding tides.

---

* For a thorough discussion of this important distinction between Anselm's Germanic idea of satisfaction *or* punishment, and our current Roman idea of satisfaction *as equal to* punishment, I would refer the theological reader to an article upon "The Roots of Anselm's Conception of Satisfaction" in the *Theologische Studien und Kritiken*, 1880, *erstes Heft.*

What we need to do is to bring all Christian facts and faiths into closest and most vital contact with our own natural habits of thought. We should wish to make Christian truths seem perfectly familiar and real in our natural ways of thought. And one glance down some line of our personal experience at the Cross of Christ, were worth more to us than any scholastic explanation of Christ's atoning sacrifice.

I shall proceed, accordingly, to indicate some personal ways in which it seems to me we may learn to enter, in some degree, into Jesus' consciousness that he must needs suffer. Yet only in some degree, and in no full measure, can we hope to comprehend in our human experience the mind that was in Jesus.

The open and most natural way of thought for us to take, in our desire to understand this most sacred truth, seems to me to be in general as follows: Let us begin by observing our own poor attempts at forgiving one another, learning what we must needs do, or suffer, in forgiving those that trespass against us, and then from our human experience dare to reason and to think up and on, Christwards and Godwards, until the love of God in Christ's atonement may seem to us the larger truth in which all our human knowledge of forgiveness is contained. Study what forgiveness of injuries involves to the most Christian man or woman, learn what forgiveness of wrong may cost the most Christlike heart, and from such knowledge gain the means of understanding why the Christ from God must needs suffer on the Cross. If we have not been compelled by some bitter experience of our own to learn the moral necessities of suffering in forgiving sin, let us search with reverent sympathies the depths of the trouble into which others have been plunged by some erring one to whom they were bound by vital ties; learn how father, mother, wife, must needs suffer in the continued charity, and shielding love, and ever open forgiveness of the home towards one who has gone forth from it, unworthy of it, and been lost in the world;—and through such experience, and such knowledge of sin and of forgiveness, and of human suffering for it beyond expression, with humble, and tender thought enter into Jesus' consciousness of us, and Jesus' knowledge of the necessity of his suffering for us, as He went to drink the cup which could not pass from him, and to give his life for ours upon the Cross.

Such in general is the vital method, the personal way, in which we may study the doctrine of the atonement of Christ for the sin of the world.

Let me briefly indicate several more definite truths which we may find in such study of the Cross.

First, In our experience of forgiveness, and its moral necessities, we find that there must be penitence or confession on the part of the person who has done wrong. We may have the disposition to forgive, we may cherish the forgiving heart, but our disposition cannot become an act of forgiveness unless there be some penitence for the wrong done, or confession of it on the part of the person who may have inflicted an injury upon us. The forgiving disposition will seek to win from another that acknowledgment; the forgiving heart will be on the watch for opportunity to exercise forgiveness; but in any true and perfect forgiveness of injury these two must always meet, the heart to forgive, and the will to confess a wrong. A broken friendship requires both for its restoration. The Christian duty is to cherish always the forgiving spirit. And the forgiving spirit will be quick to find occasion, and eager to make the most of opportunities for the exercise of forgiveness; but as the seed requires the soil in which to grow and blossom, so the forgiving spirit requires humility and penitence in the mind of another for its perfect fruit of righteousness and peace. I have known earnest-hearted people who attempted to lift themselves into unnatural and impossible virtue, because they had falsely supposed that forgiveness must be an act of free grace on their part without any relation to the mind of the recipient of it, and consequently they have struggled from a sense of duty to throw themselves into a feeling which they could not maintain without violence to other moral elements of their natures. The sense of justice and right which demands confession of wrong and restitution is as human and as divine as the love which would forgive an offense, and accept another's willingness to make restitution.

Secondly, Human forgiveness involves a painful knowledge of the wrong which has been inflicted. Forgiveness is always born of suffering. There must needs be pain and travail of soul in the birth of the forgiving spirit. You surely cannot forgive a friend if you have never known and felt the hurt of his unkindness. Your welcome would not be the hand of forgiveness extended to him, if you have not realized the wrong which he may have done your friendship. Some suffering for the injury received is an indispensable condition, or antecedent, of the exercise of forgiveness.

Thirdly, We approach now another element in the history of human forgiveness, which is of deep moral significance; viz., the suffering of the injured person must be so discovered to the wrong-doer that he can know it, and have some appreciation of it, in order that forgiveness may be granted and received, and its perfect work accomplished.

But you will ask, Is it not the glory of the forgiving spirit to hide its sense of hurt? Do we not say, Forgive and forget? Yet now you declare that the wound must be opened, and its pain made known, before there can be real forgiveness?

It is true that the sense of wrong, and the suffering for it must be forgotten at the end of the act of forgiveness, and forever afterwards. The wound must not be kept always open. Christ suffered once for all. It is the glory of forgiveness not to remember what was suffered before the friendship was restored. The forgiving heart keeps no scars. It were contrary to all charity to carry a grudge after hands have been shaken over an offense condoned. But I am not speaking of the results of forgiveness,— of its new grace and peace,—but rather of the conditions and necessities of forgiveness, or of the things indispensable to its exercise, when I say that there must needs be some revelation of the evil which has been done, and the hurt suffered, and the cost of the injustice to the person who has been aggrieved. And the human forgiveness is never more than a polite fiction, if there is not in the hour of reconciliation this frank declaration and acknowledgment of the wrong done, and the suffering received from it. Some revelation on the part of the person forgiving of the suffering which has been inflicted by the sin against him, is just as necessary to perfect forgiveness as is confession of that wrong on the part of the person who has committed it. Let either be wanting, and the reconciliation is only a truce, or a compromise, not a real and full forgiving and forgetting.

Here is a man, for example, who in his youth was thrown rudely upon the world by some one who ought to have stood by him. In consequence he lost opportunity, was put upon a hard struggle for himself, and received a wound upon his very soul, over which indeed the years of his growth have closed, and whose pain now in his better days for the most part he can forget. It is there, however, a remembered wrong, a sense of injustice which makes him quick to resent all other injustice in the world. His indignation for that sin against him is become a controlled passion, yet he knows that the fire of it is still alive at the heart of his character. Now how can that man forgive that wrong? Let the sinner against him come to him, himself perhaps after many years in need, broken down, and grown conscious of the evil he had done. Now then the injured man has the opportunity to forgive; yet the sight of that man who once wronged him, though a suppliant now and in distress, arouses the old indignation, sets again his soul aflame. He cannot help it. That sense of injustice in him makes him tremble with its passion. Yet he would forgive as he hopes to be forgiven. How can he do it, and satisfy that up-leaping justice in his own soul? How can he give his hand, and help his enemy, and forget the past, and at the same time keep the integrity of his own soul?

My friends, we have not touched the divine problem of atonement for the sin of the world unless we have honestly attempted this task of human forgiveness, unless we have sounded for others, if not for ourselves, the moral depths of this problem of a perfect human reconciliation. One thing in it seems to me clear as conscience. That wronged man cannot forgive his repentant enemy by treating his sin as though it had been nothing, by making light of it as though it had not cost him days of trouble, by hiding it in his good nature as though it were not an evil thing. Somehow that sense of injustice in his soul must find vent and burn itself out. Somehow that sense of wrong must manifest itself, and in some pure revelation of itself pass away. It cannot pass forever away except through revelation, as the fire expires through the flame. Yet in forgiveness justice must be a self-revealing flame, and not a consuming fire. Something like this has been the process of all genuine human reconciliations which I have observed. As an essential element of the reconciliation there was some revelation of pure justice. There was no hiding of the wrong. On either side there was no belittling the injury. There was no trifling with it as though a sin were nothing. It was no thoughtless forgiveness out of mere good nature, in which the heart's deeper sense of righteousness was not satisfied. When after conference, confession, and mutual revelations of mind and heart, forgiveness was bestowed and received, when the reconciliation was completed, then, if it were no superficial work, soon to be undone again, this observation I have always found to be true of it, that both parties were satisfied in it; the whole moral nature of each person rested content in the good work accomplished; nothing more was left to be remembered, explained or suffered. A personal satisfaction had been accomplished which both accepted, and on the ground of that satisfaction the friendship was resumed, the old life buried from memory, and the new life begun. Anything less than that is not perfect reconciliation between friends. Anything short of that is not complete human forgiveness. Anything less thorough than that is no foundation for a new, abiding friendship.

I have left myself time only to point to the way by which we may ascend from this our human experience of forgiveness to the Cross of Christ, and the necessity for it in the love of God. In the Person of Christ, and through the life of Christ, God has identified himself with man, made himself as far as the Infinite One may, subject to the conditions of our human experience, and our human consciousness of sin and suffering. We are so bound up with one another that every day some innocent one suffers with the guilty. It is a part of the penalty of sin that in every human transgression some just one must needs suffer with the guilty. This is a natural necessity of our human, or organic, relationship. And because we are so bound up together in good and in evil, we can bear one another's burdens, suffer helpfully for another, and to a certain extent save one another from the evil of the world. Now, according to these Gospels, God in Christ puts himself into this human relationship, and, as one with man, bears his burden and suffers under the sin of the world. The Father of spirits in his own eternal blessedness may not suffer with men; but in Christ God has humbled himself to our consciousness of sin and death. In Christ the eternal love comes under the moral law of suffering, under which forgiveness may work its perfect work.

More particularly, in the life and death of Christ these several elements which we have found belonging essentially to our experience of reconciliation with one another, have full exercise and scope. For Christ, identifying himself with our sinful consciousness, makes a perfect repentance for sin, and confession of it unto the Father. Christ experiences our sin as sinful, and confesses it. And again, Christ realizes the cost of the sin of the world. His loneliness of spirit, the cruel misunderstandings of him by all men, his Gethsemane, his Cross,—all realize the cost and suffering of sin, and in view of such sufferings of the Son of man sin never can be regarded as a light and trifling thing. And still further, Christ reveals to the world what its sin has cost, and enables man who would be forgiven to appreciate it, and to acknowledge it.

Hence as we come to the Father in the name of Christ, reading the condemnation of our sin in the life and the death of Christ, knowing how God has been aggrieved by it from the sufferings of Christ, and making our own his confession of it, there is no reason left in the nature of God why forgiveness

A Study of the Atonement. 223

should not have its perfect work, as under similar moral conditions there is no reason why we should not forgive one another. Thus, likewise, God can be satisfied in forgiving and forgetting our sins. All the moral elements and conditions necessary to reconciliation, so far as we have experience of them, and the new sympathies and fresh hopes of restored friendship, are met and satisfied in the divine forgiveness through Jesus Christ.

And we may be confident that a way of forgiveness which satisfies God himself will be sufficient to meet any demands of his law, or necessities of his moral government. God himself is his government, and is greater than his government. The moral order of this universe is expressive of the ethical nature of God. And above all it is with God himself, the righteous Father, that we have to do. Everything in the Gospel is personal.

I have tried thus to draw out from our common human experience of forgiveness, and its moral necessities, some thoughts for the study of this most sacred and spiritually difficult of themes. It is, however, a true remark that a man can understand only what he has the beginnings of in himself. From the experience which we may have begun to have of forgiving each other's trespasses, we may derive some true knowledge of the divine forgiveness of our sins. And the moral laws and moral necessities of the lower mirror "the must needs suffer" of the higher. Yet if any of you find more readily comprehensible any of the older and more familiar methods of presenting the doctrine of the atonement, use those means which are helpful to your thoughts, remembering always that they are your ways of access to the truth, and not the full measure of the truth of God's atoning love in Christ.

Beyond and above all our attempts at explaining, and our reasonings about, the death of Christ, let the Cross of Christ be to us God's sign upon our world of sin and sorrow.

We do not begin to know the depths of the love of God. Our troubles only begin to disclose to us his infinite mercies. God's love is deeper than the skies, and all-encompassing; our world in its sins, and with all its graves, lies in the infinite heaven of God's presence, and God's pure love.

XVIII.

THE GOSPEL A GIFT TO THE SENSES.

"Jesus saith unto him, Thomas, because thou hast seen me, thou hast believed: blessed are they that have not seen, and yet have believed."
—JOHN xx. 29.

THE appearance and the words of the risen Lord to Thomas disclose the lower and the higher evidence which God offers of himself to the world in Jesus Christ. The Gospel has been happily called a gift of God to the human imagination; it is also a gift of God to the human reason; but besides this the Gospel is a gift of God to the senses of man. The risen Lord on his way to the heavenly city from Jerusalem, where he had been delivered to death, was willing to be seen of men, and consented that a doubter should touch his side. The appearances of Jesus after the resurrection were all gifts of God to the senses of men. In the whole life of Jesus before his death and resurrection this same divine condescension had been manifested. There had been a continual gift of God in his teaching to the reason and the spiritual imagination of the world; and also, together with this higher revelation, running side by side with it, there had been in the visible presence on earth of the Son of man, and through his mighty works, a revelation of God to the senses of men. I wish upon this Easter morning to take for our text and our subject this lower evidence and lesser gift of God to man in the sensible revelation of God in

Jesus' human form, and especially in his appearances to men after the resurrection. I design, however, only incidentally to discuss the value of these manifestations of the risen Lord as evidence to our faith; my main object is to impress certain practical considerations which are to be derived from reflection upon this gift of God in Christ to our bodily senses.

It is precisely this lower gift of God in the physical works and manifestations of Jesus both before and after his death, which we find it most difficult to receive. Our age stumbles over the miracles of Jesus, and seeks to keep its connection with Christianity by idealising the Christ of the Gospel. The moral power of the life of Christ commands men's devotion. But the recorded gifts of God to the senses many find it difficult to receive. Thoughtful minds have sometimes accepted the miracles of Christ because they first have believed in Christ himself. Since they have been compelled to believe in the divine originality and power of Jesus himself, they believe also in his works. Because they accept the higher evidence and revelation of God in the sphere of the moral and the spiritual, they will not deny the evidence and revelation of God in the sphere of the physical and the sensible.

Sympathizing with this process of faith, I come back, however, to the gift of God through Christ's life and resurrection to the senses of man, with the conviction that it means more, and may be of more worth to us, than we often think.

When we are pressed by the difficulties of conceiving spiritual realities, we usually remind one another how partial and superficial is any knowledge of things which we can possibly gain through our bodily senses. And this superficiality and partialness of our sensible knowledge, we reflect, is increasingly apparent the farther our sciences penetrate towards the inner principles and last laws of things. None will be more disposed to admit how little he knows, than the man who has gained the largest mastery of any physical science. We can translate into our perceptions of sound, and color, and light, only a small part of the influences which we know pervade nature; and these perceptions represent only our present modes of personal contact, at a few points, with the infinite universe of God. Knowledge is always seeking to push beyond sense, and we have succeeded in naming and following many subtle essences and magnetic influences which no man hath seen, or can see. We may imagine, we cannot tell, what worlds within worlds, what spheres beyond spheres, might reveal their wonderful order and beauty to some added sense, or finer faculty of being, than we possess in our present embodiment. It is common and customary for us to remind ourselves of these limitations of sense when we would find room in nature for supernatural effects, or believe that Powers from the unseen world may have had their hours of manifestation in the history of this lower earth. All this is true, and may be profitably remembered; and such reflections are sufficient, if we would answer simply the presumption of our sensible experience against the possibility of a miracle. We should need to know vastly more than any man can know of the regions of forces and phenomena which lie just beyond the visible and beneath the tangible, before we should have reason to deny credible evidence of some event in nature which lies beyond all our experience of nature.

This often necessary and profitable view of the meagreness and limitations of our sensible knowledge is not, however, the only view of the matter to be taken. I doubt if it be on the whole the largest and truest view we may gain. For throughout the Bible, and particularly in the Gospels, there is a certain positiveness of appeal to the senses which impresses us. God in the process of revelation has honored even these imperfect and limited senses of ours. There were voices of God sounding as audible words to the prophets, and the angel of God's presence appeared before Abraham's tent; and this beginning of miracles did Jesus at Cana of Galilee; and many mighty works followed the Lord on his way of divine revelation; and after his death the stone was rolled away from before the sepulchre; and the disciples were glad when they *saw* the Lord. All the four Gospels show how carefully, with what painstaking thoughtfulness, in what convincing ways, Jesus after his resurrection, before his complete withdrawal into the glory of God's unseen presence, showed himself to the disciples, and gave the Gospel of the resurrection as a gift to their bodily senses, as well as to their reasons and their hearts.

Moreover, the emblems of his life and death for us which Jesus with so much thoughtful provision bequeathed to his disciples, indicate, in every fresh presentation of them, how Christ condescended to make his Gospel a gift even to our bodily senses. Whatever Christ took pains to do, must have real value and meaning for us, if we will receive it.

Accordingly, I would remind you, first, that the appearances of the risen Lord to the senses of the disciples are fitted to impress upon us the worth of embodiment, and of the knowledge which is gained through the body. The fact of the resurrection, as it was witnessed even to the eyes and the ears of the disciples,—the doctrine of the resurrection, as it stands upon that testimony in the creed of the Church,—is a grand affirmation of the worth of the body to the soul, and a discovery to us of a divine law of life which provides suitable embodiment for the spirit through all its ascending power, and in its final perfection. The Christian doctrine of the resurrection is a continual protest against any tendencies of thought, or habits of life, which would despise matter, or regard a human body as a worthless thing, born only of corruption and destined only to corruption. The gift of God to the senses in the life and the resurrection of Jesus Christ, honors the human eye, and the human ear, and imparts a noble worth and a holy sanctity to the embodiment of the soul. It sanctifies for us and makes honorable the whole nature-side of our existence. And you will reflect how practically important it is that we should rightly receive and value this honor which the appearance of Christ in the flesh both before and after his resurrection has placed upon the human body and its senses. The fact that Jesus rose bodily from the dead puts all sins against the body under greater condemnation, and it raises also to a Christian duty not only the proper care of the body, but also the culture of the physical faculties, and the training of the soul for contact with divinity through its physical powers of apprehension.

The distrust which good men have often felt of all knowledge, refreshment of soul, or enjoyment, which may come to us through the eye or the ear, or in the study of outward things, or by means of any of the influences of nature upon the soul through its material organism, is a failure to honor the body as God honored it when He took upon himself the form of man, when Christ worked in the realm of physical processes, and when he consented to be seen and to be touched by doubting disciple. The resurrection of Christ and its revelation of our continued embodiment in forms more celestial, discloses not only the worth of this body, but also the value of all acquisitions which we may now gain in these bodies and through their faculties of perception. Whatever you may learn through the training of any power of observation, or in the perfection of any physical faculty, is a clear gain of soul for its immortal existence. All physical culture and acquisition may have significance beyond itself. In a higher sense than the ancients knew we may learn to paint for eternity, or to sing for immortality, for all knowledge gained through these senses is true knowledge, and we shall not have to unlearn it, but rather to enlarge and perfect it, as after death and the resurrection we shall pass on in better embodiment to larger studies and finer knowledge of the creative thoughts of the Eternal. For us to despise the body, or to ignore the physical elements of life and knowledge, would be to undervalue the significance of God's gift of his Son to the eyes of the disciples, and to the touch of Thomas.

The pages of religious biography abound with illustrations of the misunderstanding or neglect of the Gospel of Christ to the senses. Religion has sometimes seemed afraid of nature, and has hesitated to enjoy the whole pure nature-side of faith. Thus the early Church was betrayed into a wasteful and cruel asceticism by the pagan error of thinking that God can be found only in the farthest spiritual realms, and that the life of man in nature is something common and unclean. And that old falsehood has lingered and lurked in Christian thought until this day, to taint and to spoil not a few of the good gifts of God to men. A similar hard error in medieval theology drove a sharp distinction between nature and grace, and the Roman church divorced these two helpmeets of life which God has joined together, and which the Son of man did not put asunder. The result was to debase a considerable portion of man's natural activity as something beneath moral attention; and also, in consequence of this separation between nature and grace, the Church first neglected, then suspected, and then persecuted, the natural sciences. The evil of this neglect and contempt for the natural has been felt not only in an enforced opposition between religion and science, but also in the loss from Christian thought and life of certain healthful and helpful elements of faith which God is always ready to impart through natural influences, and to a sincere and humble love of nature. It would be an interesting study to inquire how far the reformed theology, with all its massive strength, lost grace and restfulness, and warm color, from that lack of appreciation of God's thought in nature which characterized generally the literature of the seventeenth and eighteenth centuries. The sublime doctrine of God's high decrees might have been presented with less forbidding sternness, and have seemed more habitable for men, had there been more love of nature, and of the least flower by the wayside, in the hearts of the Genevan reformers; had travellers in those days not been wont to regard the Alps simply as obstacles to be crossed, and had they lingered in those valleys of loveliness guarded by white thrones of Deity. Calvinism, it has often been observed, lacked humanness and naturalness—a lack less felt in Martin Luther's sermons; and Luther, we know, loved children, and his writings contain more reference to common natural things than the other reformers were wont to make. Jonathan Edwards, in one of his meditations, seemed at a loss to account for the spiritual influence which had led him to take delight in the stern doctrine of God's sovereignty, which in his earlier years had repelled and disheartened him. But when we read of his walks upon the banks of the Hudson, and of his communings with God in the quiet forests, whose shadows are shot through with the sunbeams, and where the rocks are covered with mosses, and nature finds place to hang her grasses and blue-bells in the clefts of the crags, it is not a far fancy to suppose that the influence of the Holy Spirit in the Gospel of nature to the senses of Edwards may have worked more subtly than he

The Gospel a Gift to the Senses. 233

knew in causing the higher and holiest revelations of the Divine glory to seem to him unspeakably attractive and lovable.

Indeed with reference to the whole nature-side of religion the words of the Lord Jesus are a constant suggestion and lesson to faith. I venture to say that more allusions to natural objects, to the lilies, the birds of the air, the vine, the trees, the grass, the white harvest-fields, the abundant fruit, the waters of the lake, and the solitary places of the mountains, are to be found within the compass of these brief Gospels than may be discovered in whole tomes of Thomas Aquinas, or in the Institutes of Calvin. Jesus came to fulfill, not to destroy, and that men might have life abundantly. It is interesting to reflect that the Son of man lived with his disciples for the most part out of doors, under the open sky, in the fisher's boat, on the other side of the lake among the mountains, or walking day after day in the quiet ways between the towns and the villages of Galilee. Jesus trained his disciples for the most part in the country, by the lake, and in the wilderness; he went up to the city to be crucified by the sins of men. It is not irreverent to think of Jesus as a true child of nature as he was the Son of man; for both nature and humanity come from God and are of God. The parables and the teaching of Jesus are pervaded by a divine naturalness, a simple truthfulness and healthfulness, which the Church too soon lost in its asceticism, and scholasticism forgot in its labored divinity, which the reformed theology was slow to regain, and which we often miss in our artificialities and fictitiousness of religious manners and life. Our Christian thought needs to honor and to love the truth of God in nature, in the least things of God in the fields, and in our ever fresh discoveries of His works, in order that we may know better and keep truly the revelation of God in his grace. Everything unnatural is really un-Christian. " I should like to see before I die," so Thackeray wrote in one of his lately published letters, " and think of it daily more and more, the commencement of Jesus Christ's christianism in the world. . . . We are taught to be ashamed of our best feelings all our life."

There might have been less reason for this reproach of the kindly humanist, had Christian thought always been possessed with a truer sense of the value which God has placed in the person of Christ, and by his resurrection, upon this human body and all the life of nature into which the spirit is born and baptized through its embodiment. Thackeray recalls a thought too often missing from our reasonings concerning foreknowledge and decrees, when he writes in the same letter, "An angel glorified or a sparrow on a gutter are equally parts of His creation. The light upon all the saints in Heaven is just as much and no more God's work, as the sun which shall shine to-morrow upon this infinitesimal speck of creation, and under which I shall read, please God, a letter from my kindest Lady and friend." Ruskin's remark is profoundly true that under similar circumstances he that has the most love of nature will have the most faith in God. Is it saying too much to affirm that distrust of any natural law is unbelief, and denial of any scientific fact is atheism? Any thought or habit which dishonors the body, or disdains the Gospel of God's truth to the senses of man, despises also the temple of God, and contemns the holy presence of the Creator. "What?" said an indignant Apostle, "know ye not that your body is the temple of the Holy Ghost which is in you, which ye have of God, and ye are not your own?"

By putting such emphasis upon the natural even in the name of him who was crucified, do you mean, then, to make a religion of natural instinct? to tell young men to follow their healthful natural impulses, and be saved? Surely not that. Nature is not yet conscience. And there are fires of unnatural passion which sin has kindled in the veins of man. Sin has also become incarnate in this flesh, and must be crucified. But I mean that in the kingdom of grace nature is to be owned, consecrated, sanctified, blessed. I mean that the natural is for the spiritual, as well as the spiritual for the natural. I mean that each shall be perfected with the other in the kingdom of redemption. The gift of God to the senses in the bodily form, the miracles of healing, and the resurrection of Jesus, reveal the truth that the full and final life for the children of God will not be a solitary life of pure spirit, unembodied, and without participation in the beauty and the joy of all this "mighty world of sound and sense," but that it shall be the perfect reconciliation and immortal harmony of nature and spirit, of sense and soul, of our inward consciousness of thought and love, and all outward things.

Yet there is one further question which thrusts itself upon us, the old question which in times past has led men to shrink from this body, and from contact with matter as though it were a curse;—the question how can this fire of sin in our veins be quenched, how can we be freed from temptation, sickness, pain, the darkening of the light of the spirit within us, and death, unless we escape wholly from imprisonment in this material element, and live as pure spirits before God? And when you dwell upon the healthfulness of nature, and of delight of soul in it, and of its enlarging and softening influence upon our thoughts of the Father of all, are you not forgetting the evil of it, the dark side of it, "the mountain's gloom," as well as "the mountain's glory?" Do you remember how many there are to whom their bodies are life-long afflictions? how many who carry about with them daily some thorn in the flesh? how many to whom embodiment means confinement for years in a single chamber of sickness? and how for all of us nature under the curse of sin goes trembling down to the grave?

My friends, we can none of us forget these facts of sin, and death; they are always before us. The shadow of them lies across our whole life from the cradle to the grave. Nevertheless, this evil aspect of things is but the half truth, a shadow thrown athwart life, not the whole revelation of God to us. Death is not the whole, or final truth of life. For a lifeless body seems to be not only a denial of man's free spirit, but a mockery of nature also. Was it for that, nature's noblest work was fashioned? Was it for that, the most repulsive of all corruption, that her finest elements were mixed, her subtlest essences compounded, her power of organization carried to its last degree of intricacy and complexity? Truly, if a dead body were the end of embodiment, nature would be from the beginning to the end of her work one awful lie. If the dead body in the grave were the end of human embodiment, health is a mockery, delight in nature an irony, all our acquisition of knowledge of the world and the stars a hopeless folly, and that growth and culture of spirit which we gain through the training of eye or ear, or the skillful use of our hands, were a vain and profitless task. *If* the dead body be the end of human embodiment! You say you find it difficult to conceive of the resurrection, and of bodies celestial; but think how much more difficult it is to conceive that this body which dies is to be the end of all God's great thought of human embodiment, of all life of the immortal spirit in contact with nature, in perception of the harmonies of the spheres, in sight of the glory of God's infinite creation! It is against nature to imagine that a dead body must be an end—death a blank wall at the close—of God's way of embodiment. Were there no gift of the Gospels to the senses we still should find our life here in nature, and for nature, a prophetic life. It contains in itself the earnest expectation of the creature for the manifestation of the sons of God.

Thus we are led to the second great truth which was attested by the appearances of the risen Lord;—our present bodies are preparatory and prophetic forms of embodiment. They are predictions of something better to come. They are preparations for future embodiment. And the fact of the resurrection is a revelation to us of this complete truth, that God has made us to live in nature, and in happy contact with things natural, and also that in our present bodily existence we do but begin to be what we shall be when God's whole thought of us as embodied souls shall be at length fully developed, and confirmed in our eternal life.

In this world we can take cognizance of the human body only in its first growth and its imperfect fitness to our spiritual powers. Then, when it reaches its full stature, and its utmost draft of vitality upon the material forces of this earth is exhausted, it returns to earth, and we know not whence its animating principle has fled. Jesus Christ, in those days between the morning when he rose from the dead, and the hour of his final disappearance, exemplified and illustrated a still further continuation and development of the divine law of spiritual embodiment, for he discovered to the senses of his disciples a risen body, which was still like the human form that they had known, and yet which was unlike this body of flesh; it came and went; it appeared and disappeared, as a form belonging to some higher order, and freed from the compulsions of corruptible matter. And towards the close of that interval of forty days the body of Jesus seemed to become even more spiritual, and less like the forms of this earthliness, and we read of his last appearance to the eleven in Galilee upon a mountain, that when they saw him they worshipped, but some doubted. Already the embodiment of the Holy One, whom God would not suffer to see corruption, was being carried on and up into forms spiritual and celestial beyond the power of human eye to see, or human hand to touch; and

The Gospel a Gift to the Senses.

when at last the earthly was laid aside, and the resurrection was completed in the glorified humanity of Jesus, he ascended from them, and came back no more to be seen of men. The record of the Gospel to the senses was finished, and the dispensation of the Spirit followed according to His promise.

XIX.

THE LIMITS OF SPIRITUAL MANIFESTATION.

"This is now the third time that Jesus was manifested to the disciples, after that he was risen from the dead."—JOHN xxi. 14.

"And it came to pass, while he blessed them, he parted from them, and was carried up into heaven."—LUKE xxiv. 51.

I WISH to speak this morning concerning the manifestation of divine and spiritual things. We often wish that they could become more apparent to men. We wonder why so much of the Gospel is left to faith, why more of God's glory is not given to sight. I think it may prove helpful to bring out into clear declaration some of these spiritual disappointments which shadow sometimes the faith of ordinary Christians. We find it difficult to realize spiritual things. We look at death, and say one to another under our breath, No man knows. The thought will come unbidden, since there is a God, as man must believe, why does God not impress himself with visible evidence upon us? If there be a city of God, why do its inhabitants never appear, coming and going, through the atmosphere of this earth? If the Lord be risen indeed, why should not each generation have its manifestation of his presence? Why are we left to wonder, to reason, and to preach? Why are men left at liberty to believe, or to eke out their lives as best they may in unbelief, when it would seem as though the Christ who showed himself to the disci-

Limits of Spiritual Manifestation. 241

ples might manifest himself by visible signs from heaven, and God be revealed with demonstration to the senses so convincing that every man must see him, and cry out, What must I do to be saved?

I ask these questions because I think that we may obtain some partial answer to them, and because I believe that it is always the truest and wisest thing for us to take the secret questionings of our thoughts out into the open, and to look all around them, and to go on our way.

The season also of the Church year after Easter and before the ascension and Pentecost, naturally suggests the inquiry, How did Jesus manifest himself to the disciples, and why did he cease manifesting himself after forty days? For this is the remarkable fact of history, according to these Gospels, that our Lord after the resurrection could appear to the disciples for a period of forty days apparently at his own will, and that then He ascended from them beyond either his power, or his will to manifest himself again sensibly to them; and since that brief season of his manifestation no man of all the doubting or tried or sorrowful ones in this world has ever seen the Lord.

There must be some reason for this. There must be some law in it. We cannot admit that anything in revelation is accidental. We cannot suppose that anything supernatural is capricious or lawless. There must be one divine order of this universe including both the supersensible and the sensible, the supernatural and the natural, and all the relations and interactions of the two. Jesus' manifestations of himself, therefore, after his resurrection must have followed some law of revelation, and his ceasing to show himself to the disciples must also be in accordance with some law of nature and of God. In other words there must have been some reasons why he could show himself to the disciples as he did during those forty days, and why afterwards he could not manifest himself as he has not done during these eighteen centuries. Perhaps if we could discover some hint, or follow a little ways some suggestion of this law of God's revelation and God's withdrawal of himself from us, we might find our faith greatly helped and strengthened. For this purpose I must ask thoughtful attention while I offer some ideas which seem to me tenable.

Let us begin with the side of this subject which lies nearest at hand, and then follow it out in the direction of our present inquiry.

Consider, first, how the spirit which is in man manifests itself, and what the limits of our spirits are in showing themselves. The life of man is a manifestation of his soul, yet it is a partial, imperfect manifestation of it, having certain fixed limits. All parents know how interesting—what a daily wonder,—is the process by which from infancy the mind of a child begins to disclose itself. Could we understand better that common daily miracle of the manifestation of mind in the growth of the new born child, we should solve many a hard question of the philosophers. But the one always impressive thing is, that in a body and through a life something unseen, imponderable, in its spiritual essence unknown, comes to manifestation, discloses its personality, makes itself a felt and influential presence amid the facts and forces of this

Limits of Spiritual Manifestation. 243

world. Every human life is a revelation of soul. Spirit is showing itself in every kindling eye, and through each living voice. But this is not all. The manifestation of spirit in body can be carried only to a certain extent. Soon a limit is reached which cannot be passed. Some faces may bring more spirit to manifestation than others; some lives may be more tremulous with soul than others; but all find in the body a limit, as well as a means, of manifestation. Earthly matter can receive and express only so much of spirit; the *overplus* of soul, if any there be, remains unmaterialized, unexpressed. Indeed there is more every day in human thought than can ever get itself into definite speech; there is more in human love than can be revealed by look or word or gift. The spirit which is in man is never fully manifested in these bodies, is never wholly revealed in things seen and present. There is more soul in humanity than has ever shown itself in history. The electricity which is seen in the flashes of the cloud is but a moment's visibility, at a single point, of the pervasive electric power with which this earth is charged. The history of humanity is overcharged with spirit. What has thus far come to manifestation in art, in literature, in achievement, is but as the flash in the cloud. If common matter cannot possibly bring to manifestation all of the subtle magnetic forces with which it is pervaded, still less can things seen and tangible bring to revelation the Spirit and the Divinity with which the creation is vivified and inspired.

I have been dwelling upon this thought because it is necessary to our purpose that we should perceive clearly this general law of spiritual revelation, and its limits; viz.: Our human spirits can manifest themselves in bodily forms, and be thus seen and known of men; but this manifestation has certain fixed limits in the nature of matter beyond which it cannot possibly be carried. Now it seems to me that in this simple general statement we have a very useful and helpful hint for our understanding of God's revelation of himself to us. The creation is a manifestation of something beyond sense and sound. Science speaks of all outward things as phenomena, things which do appear, not things which are. Nature is appearance of some Power behind nature, as a human face is expression of some spirit or character beneath it. All outward nature is a suggestion of some intelligence. Hills and clouds, trees and flowers, all these endless combinations of elementary forms in nature, are symbols, types, means of expression in what, with the simplest as well as profoundest science, we call the book of nature. Hence we speak of nature as a revelation of God. It is the oldest Testament, and to all honest, devout minds a sacred Scripture. So Kepler the astronomer read God's thoughts after him in the laws of the planetary motions. True science is a discovery of some higher order of things than seem to be.

Then, besides this manifestation of God in nature, we read the record in human history of some higher providence than man's wisdom. Exactly as a human life from youth to manhood, and in the achievements of its maturity, brings the spirit of a man to revelation, so that by the life and its works we know the man, so human history taken as one whole, the life of humanity in its progress and destiny, seems to discover to our knowledge some Power greater than man, and a Providence which imparts unity and continuity to man's history. And the particular line along which this revelation of God has been clearest, most impressive, and purest, has been in the historic line from Moses to Christ, and on in the spiritual power and progress of Christianity.

In the life of Jesus Christ the revelation of God has reached its intensest, whitest light. All manifestations of Spirit and of God seem to have culminated in the person of Christ. Read the life of Christ even before his crucifixion and resurrection, and it seems at times as though this earth could not hold so much of divinity. When Jesus speaks some of those gloriously new words, when he is doing some of those wonderfully gracious acts, it seems as if the Divineness within him would consume its veil of flesh in the brightness of its manifestation. The transfiguration upon that holy mount is what might have been expected at any moment of the ministry of such a Being, so luminous with God. On the shore of the lake, on the mountain as he blesses the people, in the way up to Jerusalem with the disciples, in the Temple among the rulers, there is such a glory of God coming to expression in his teachings, such a wonder of divinity in his manner and his speech, such a fullness of the presence of God in his person, that the earthly and the human shine and burn, and almost give way and vanish in the transcendence of his Spirit. The transfiguration is the *overplus* of Divinity, the unrevealable glory of the Father in the Son of God, surcharging even his raiment, and transforming for a moment the face of Jesus and enveloping disciples in its overawing light.

Surely we draw near the fullest human disclosure of God, and the last possible limits of divine revelation, when at length we see such a Man as Jesus had shown himself to be taking up his cross, accepting death, giving his life for the world. Love—the divinest thing in all the universe to be revealed—manifests its glory, the glory of the Father, in the ministry unto death of the Son of man. "Greater love hath no man than this, that a man lay down his life for his friends." How can God's love find intenser manifestation than in the Life of the Son of his love, who gave himself for us all?

Had the Gospels stopped with the account of the crucifixion, had God shown himself to us men only in the sinless life, and the sacrificial death of Jesus, and left only the record of his works, his teachings, and his Person more marvelous than all his works, for our faith and hope, still we should have had reason to believe in him as the Messiah, and believing in him to live true, manly lives here in the hope of some still better life beyond. We might have said, even had the Gospels stopped at the Cross, "Truly this was the Son of God." We might have thought that God had manifested himself in Jesus to the utmost, and that we must needs go ourselves beyond death in order to become able to receive more spiritual discoveries of God's presence.

But mercifully, condescendingly to our great human need of signs and evidence of divinity, God in Christ, according to these Gospels, has carried the manifestation of the spiritual yet one moment and degree further in the realm of the visible and sensible. We read, "This is now the third time that Jesus was manifested to the disciples, after that he was risen from the dead." There is an accuracy of detail, a perfectness of simplicity, and withal a reserve and absence of excitement or exaggeration about this chapter of John's Gospel which greatly impresses us with its truthfulness. The art of the narrative is too perfect to be art. It is a mirror of reality. "Simon Peter saith unto them, I go a fishing." There can be no doubt that Peter said that. The other disciples naturally say, "We also go with thee," and "they went forth, and entered into the boat; and that night they took nothing." They were perhaps too bewildered, purposeless, absent-minded men, to notice what they were doing that night on the lake, or to go and find where the great schools of fish might be breaking. It was the hour when the day was dawning; and they saw a form, which they did not at first glance recognize, of one standing on the shore. He told them where to cast the net; and it is true that John with his quick instinct of love divined instantly before the keen eyes of Peter had discerned that it was the Lord.

And Peter threw himself into the water and struck out vigorously, Peter-like, for the shore; and the other disciples,—we can see it all,—did not stop to sweep the larger boat from its anchorage in upon the beach, but "came in the little boat (for they were not far from the land, but about two hundred cubits off), dragging the net full of fishes." The fire of coals, the fish laid thereon, and bread, Simon Peter going up to draw the net to land, and counting the fishes, the exact number being a hundred and fifty and three, and all large;—all these minute particulars and details of the sacred narrative are taken from memory, just as they must have happened; there is the unconscious truthfulness of an eye-witness in all this.

But what of the divine manifestation? There is no description given of Jesus' appearance although these little natural details of the scene are reproduced so exactly. His words are repeated, Christlike words, like Him who spake as never man spake, words which are so Christlike that we know disciple never invented or could have imagined them; but the manifestation of the presence of the risen Lord, how he came, and went, how he appeared,—there is no description attempted of that. It is simply affirmed and attested that it was the Lord, and that this was the third time he was manifested. We have the record of two other appearances of the risen Lord, and then the limit is reached, and the Lord has become too transcendent and divine to be seen again in bodily manifestation by his disciples. "And it came to pass, while he blessed them, he parted from them, and was carried up into heaven." Henceforth they shall not meet him in Galilee. They must follow him beyond death to see him again, and to be forever with the Lord.

In the appearances of Jesus after death we have the manifestation of that which is spiritual and divine carried to its last degree of earthly possibility. These material conditions can reveal so much of the spiritual, and no more. Matter would break down under more spiritual pressure. Earthly elements

Limits of Spiritual Manifestation. 249

would dissolve in intenser radiance of divinity. There is a limit in the nature of the carbon point even for the power of electricity to show itself. The incandescence may be too great for the point of manifestation, and both disappear. There is a limit in the nature of the spirit beyond which it must fail to become apparent to the disciples' senses. In the appearances of Jesus after death the power of the spiritual to reveal itself seems to be nearing its utmost limit. One step further into the spiritual realm, and Jesus himself will become invisible. One more manifestation, and the limits of nature's power to show Divinity will be reached. One more gracious and commanding revelation to the eleven of the glory of the risen Lord, and the end of the whole history of Divine manifestations will be gained, the risen Lord will pass henceforth beyond the powers of our mortality to apprehend his presence, and He will be with us always in his Spirit.

If you have followed me thus far along this line of thought, these further reflections will now be in place, and may prove clearing of doubts, and helpful to faith.

First, We observe that everything in the life of Christ,—his nativity, his divine teachings, his miracles, his obedience unto death, his resurrection, his appearances after the resurrection, his ascension,—all are in accordance with a law of divine revelation. These are not arbitrary, accidental, unaccountable events, contrary to experience, but they fall in with and constitute one law and history, one order and purpose of God's self-revelation even to the uttermost to us men. I will not delay to illustrate or enforce this; I leave the suggestion of it to some doubting minds with the remark that when we fairly grasp the idea of a divine law of revelation running through the whole creation, and reaching its highest power in Jesus and the resurrection, we have seized upon a principle of reasonable faith which lifts us above a thousand difficulties and objections.

Secondly, It is comforting and assuring for any man of us to reflect that one reason why we have to believe so much, and can see so little, is simply because there are such glorious and divine things to be revealed that they cannot possibly be manifested to our bodily senses. Too dazzling light would consume the eye uplifted to it. And I want to enforce this remark.

A man is active, full of life and spirit, and he dies. We can see no more manifestation of him. He has gone from us. What is the reason that we cannot see him, or hear him, or meet him? Why does he not come back and counsel us and comfort us? We never needed him more. Ah! my friends,—what is this law of spiritual manifestation and its necessary limits? Have we not been remembering that spirit is greater than matter, soul diviner than body, and that spirit by its very essence and fineness of being may easily pass on wholly into the invisible? may reach a point of love and life, of joy and purity, beyond further contact with this mortality, and hence beyond possibility of our recognition? If any departed spirits still have power to enmesh themselves in gross matter, must they not be still earthly, sensual—gross demons—not pure, free spirits? For if any pure spirits have power to come back and be

Limits of Spiritual Manifestation. 251

seen again on earth, none surely of all who have vanished into the unseen and holy would have more desire and more will to appear again, than would Christ. He knows all our need and grief. He loves his disciples to the end. Surely if any spirit can return, it will be the Lord. He first will show himself, for his love is greatest. I will wait for his appearing. I will listen to no others, until he comes. I must see the Lord first. I remember how the Christ lingered, as long as the risen Christ might, within the confines of this world, appearing for forty days to his disciples; but at length even the Christ came to the end of his power of possible manifestation to us men in these mortal bodies, on this side death. Christ in his risen and spiritual body became, at last, in the blessed ascent of his life to God, so remote from earthly temptation and touch of pain, so transcendent and glorified, that while the disciples were gazing up into heaven he vanished from them, not in the long centuries to come again until this world-age shall reach its appointed end, and these elements be dissolved in the brightness of the manifestation of the presence of the Lord.

A man, we are observing, full of soul and spiritual power, more than life has measured, dies. We say, We do not know. One thing, however, we do know. If there is any truth in science, forces do not suddenly end in nothingness. In some forms they are continued and conserved. We cannot conceive that spiritual and personal forces are exceptions to all that we know of force and its conservation. Somehow, somewhere, in some future possibilities and powers, that personal life-force goes on and on. The only question is, In what form does it continue, or with what body does it come? And the appearances of Jesus after death answer sufficiently for us that question. The manifestation of the risen Lord shows that personal force goes on after death as personal force. The manifestation of Jesus to the disciples leaves many questions unanswered which we are curious to ask, but it reveals personality continuing in a higher order of existence as personality. It was *Jesus* who was manifested. The beloved disciple knew that it was his Lord who stood, while the day was breaking, upon the shore. The disciples are as sure that it is the Lord as they are certain that there were taken in the net a hundred and fifty and three great fishes—and no break to be found in any of the meshes of the net!

We do not really need to be assured of anything further. This is enough; " It is the Lord !" Master, it is thou! Friend, it is thou! Father, mother, husband, wife, child beloved, it is thou!

In the Christian knowledge of the life which is to be revealed, we can wait yet a little while for the manner and the time of its manifestation. It is only a question of manifestation. It is not a question of reality, or existence, but only a question of manifestation of whatever is of the spirit and of God. This world manifests the divine somewhat,—all the spiritual light that can work through the thick meshes of matter; all of the divine presence that a material network of forces can be charged with; all of the influences of angels that dull human brains can be made to feel; all celestial sympathies and love this earth can know. But this little world cannot con-

Limits of Spiritual Manifestation. 253

tain it all. The fragrance cannot all be held in the flower's cup. Spirit transcends matter. There is more to be revealed. The manifestation is not over. The revelation of God has but just begun in this world, it will be continued in a better. " Howbeit that is not first which is spiritual, but that which is natural; then that which is spiritual. The first man is of the earth, earthy: the second man is of heaven. As is the earthy, such are they also that are earthy: and as is the heavenly, such are they also that are heavenly. And as we have borne the image of the earthy, we shall also bear the image of the heavenly." "When Christ, who is our life, shall be manifested, then shall ye also with him be manifested in glory."

XX.

THE INTERDEPENDENCE OF ALL SAINTS.

"And these all, having had witness borne to them through their faith, received not the promise, God having provided some better thing concerning us, that apart from us they should not be made perfect."
—HEBREWS xi. 39–40.

YEARS ago rows of elms were planted on either side of the street upon which stands our church. Each elm was a separate, isolated thing. It was to grow as straight as it might from its own individual root. But when the trees had reached their full height, and each trunk had become strong and large, the branches of the separate elms began to touch in the upper air, and their symmetrical tops cast down upon these paths the friendly shadows of meeting boughs and leaves interwoven across the sky. And long ere this, too, I suppose, the single roots which struck down into the deeper soil have formed a living net-work in the common ground, and may share the same raindrops in their interlacing life. The growth of these elms is a parable of the growth of truths in human institutions. Single ideas take root in history. A separate truth gains firm possession of some ground prepared for its reception. And opposite it another idea is implanted in history. Let the growth of either become stunted, and they will remain opposite and separate truths. But let each reach its full and perfect development, leave both alone until they have time to grow into large symmetry, and they will

The Interdependence of all Saints. 255

begin to meet above, and to draw their ample life from the same springs below. And so it happens that while hardly two hundred and fifty years ago our forefathers left the whole calendar of the saints behind them and planted upon this spot a separate church, as though it were the year one of Christian history, and all things were to be made new,—to-day, this All Saints' day, a child of the Puritans, whose are the fathers, finds his thoughts easily intertwining with thoughts that have grown from a different stock, and we perceive that the separateness which was our fathers' strength has become, in its larger growth, graceful fellowship with other communions from which they stood apart. Here in a historic church, beneath which lie buried the bones of many a stalwart Puritan whose spirit we believe is still marching on abreast with the years of God, we now without fear of the superstitions from which our fathers fled, and in the exercise of the Christian liberty which they won, may observe Christmas, and Easter, and Good Friday, and many a holy-day of the ancient Church. All Saints' day was first commemorated in the Eastern Church whose noble witnesses and martyrs were many times more in number than the days of the year; afterwards, and at a different season, it became a festival in the Western Church; and many pious and reverent believers, in several Protestant communions, at this harvest time of the year, delight to keep this day sacred to the thought and the memory of that great multitude whom no man can number, of all nations, and kindreds, and tongues,—the souls of all saints. which are the Lord's harvest from the ages of our human history.

In order that we also may enter into the associations of All Saints' day, let us suffer our thoughts to take the hint and to run gladly forth in the direction which is indicated by the Scripture chosen for our text: "They apart from us should not be made perfect." The Apostle had been speaking of the saints of the Old Testament. He had been building, in that famous chapter, the triumphal arch of Old Testament history. The names of the world's spiritual conquerors are written there. But at the close of this triumphal commemoration you cannot fail to notice the unexpected turn of the text. The conclusion towards which this whole chapter of faith's heroism seems to move would be an ascription of our indebtedness to these valiant servants of the Lord who "have made it a world for us." Without them, the writer of this sacred history would naturally have said, Without them we are not made perfect. But instead he said, "That apart from us they should not be made perfect."

The generations of the past were not made perfect without the generation to which Christ's Apostle spoke. The last living generation was in some way necessary for the perfection of all the generations which had been upon the earth. We hardly transcend the text, we do but follow the inspired word out to its larger revelation, when we say, Each Christian generation is necessary to all before; the last saint belongs in some measure to the first; the better thing of each age is for all who have lived and died; not only is it true that we inherit the lives of the saints, but they also are to inherit ours; we are for them as well as they for us; neither they nor we are to be made perfect apart; the last century of human history shall crown all the centuries; the consummation of the world is the perfection together of all the saints.

This is hardly our customary thought of the saints. We think of them as passed beyond all participation in this world's history, withdrawn from its trials and having no concern henceforth in its warfare and victories; made perfect in their own pure hearts, and their lives elsewhere no more bound up with this world's destiny. We remember with grateful love what they have been to us in the years gone by; we remind one another in our public places of our common inheritance in the lives of good men; we build monuments to the memory of the brave who died for their country; we draw inspiration for youth from the illumined historic page, and the spirit of the martyrs blends still with all sacrifice of love. But while we remember these worthy and sainted ones, we should not forget that we too are to be for them, as they have been for us; that Moses and Elias are not perfect apart from Peter and John in the presence of the Christ of the ages; that James waits for Irenæus, and Paul for Luther; that Augustine and Calvin are not perfect without Edwards and Maurice; that these all wait for some better thing which God hath provided concerning us; that we too are dependent upon our children, and our children's children, for the fullness of our lives, and the completion of our work; that all the saints from all the ages are for one another; that not in solitary glory of martyrdom, nor in singular beauty of grace, nor yet in separate happiness, nor upon any throne apart, is the saint of God to be made perfect; but, in the mutual triumphs and in the living interdependencies of the Lord Christ's kingdom, all are to be made perfect together when the city of God shall come. Let us dwell now upon this truth awhile.

Let it be known that this truth of the mutual dependence of the saints of all ages is a Biblical conception—one which we ought not to lose.

If you contemplate, for example, any sacred character from the Old Testament, you will observe that such character is never held apart either from the men of God who went before it, or from the servants of the Lord who are to follow after it. Each of these characters is put in the Bible into relation with all before and all after it—as a link in a chain; all personages that carry on God's gracious revelation, are as links in one continuous chain,—and both ends of this unbroken chain of sacred history, running through the ages, with its many links of lives interlocked in one purpose of redemption, are bound to the throne of God,—the beginning of it by the first divine act of creation, and the final end of all in the glory of the Son of man at the right hand of the majesty on high.

The interdependence of all saints, the living and the dead, and those who are to be, appears in certain events in the life of Christ, and may be inferred also from certain inspired hints in the apostolic writings. It is clear from the narrative of the transfiguration, that Moses and Elias had not been cut off by death from personal interest and anticipation in the progress of God's kingdom on earth. Moses upon the Holy Mount was as real a figure in our human history as he was upon Mount Nebo, when he stood looking toward the promised land. And Elias was still as really a character of our human history, when he became visible in Christ's transfigured presence, as he was when he waited for the appearance of the cloud which should bring heaven's blessing to the parched fields of Israel. Whatever may have been their work, or rest, in their intermediate life, Moses and Elias certainly were not removed by death beyond personal share and part in the ministry of our Lord, and personal sympathy and hope in the progress and triumph of redeeming love upon this earth. What was done here upon a place called Golgotha, was to be done for them also there in that place called Paradise. And it is deeply significant and suggestive that the apostle Peter who was one of the two to witness this revealed intimacy of the saints of the Old and the New, and to see upon the Holy Mount this close contiguity of two worlds, is the same apostle who has dropped in his epistle quite incidentally, and as a matter of course, that word which we have practically left out of our Protestant Bibles concerning Christ's preaching to the spirits in prison, and again concerning the preaching to those that are dead. I am drawing no doubtful inferences, I am indulging in no new speculations, I am simply asserting what fidelity to the Scriptures compels us to believe, and what the early church found room for in its ampler creed, when I say that Christ descended into Hades, and that he did the work appointed of the Father for him in that hour there among the dead, and that the fact of Christ's descent into Hades, upon the very day between his death and his resurrection for us, reveals some near relation between the two worlds, this earth and Hades. The Lord's life here, and the life of the dead there, were and are correlated; the history of the two spheres, the realm of the dead, and the kingdom of God on earth, were and are in some way connected and parallel histories; the two lands are contiguous, and One Lord passes back and forth across their boundary-line, to-day in the body, to-morrow in the spirit, and the third day risen again, and seen by the disciples; and he has the same administration of perfect justice and grace in both worlds. This much is not theory, but Biblical fact. We may deny utterly the fact of this revelation, if we will; but if we believe the Scripture, we should accept this fact of the dependence of both worlds upon Christ, and his activity in both, as it has been revealed to us, and we ought not to dwarf any inspired Scripture, to the low stature of some human system of theology, or seek to crush its vaster truth into any of our little theories of God's government.

These two facts at which we have just glanced, namely the part taken by Moses and Elias upon the mount of transfiguration, and the fact of Christ's descent into Hades and his activity there in the Spirit, while his body lay in the tomb awaiting the resurrection, are sufficient to show that the two realms—the one where the dead are living, and this other where we are dying—are not so far apart, are not altogether separate realms in God's government and purpose, have correlations more intimate and vital than we know; "that they apart from us should not be made perfect."

This truth of the mutual life and interdependence of all saints appears further from the whole manner and tendency of the New Testament in its treatment of the subject of death. There is hardly anything more contrary to Scripture than is our common exaggeration of the importance of death. Do we not remember how Jesus seemed always to be putting death into the background as a very secondary and even incidental thing in the history of a soul which has attained the true, the eternal life? He minimized death when he called it a sleep. We magnify it when we call it destiny. The Apostles, catching Jesus' diviner tone, called sin death, and love life. Death in the Apostolic speech was turned into a metaphor; it served to illustrate something far greater and more important than itself. Conversion to them was the great change; to die may be the greatest event which can happen to a man; but to die is one of the least important things which a man does; to repent of sin, to surrender to God, to live unto Christ,—this is the great thing for a man to do. We think of death as a vast gulf between friends; as a great barrier between hearts that would go on loving and being loved forever; as a wall of adamant suddenly reared by a divine decree between mother and child, husband and wife; and with the years the great silence widens between men and women who were friends. But when one who had been taught of Jesus has occasion to refer to death, he thinks not of chasm or adamantine wall, but of the veil of the temple—the mere veil between the holy, and the holiest place. "And this hope," he said, "enters within the veil."

> "No adamant between us uprears its rocky screen ;
> A veil before us only ;—thou in the light serene.
> That veil 'twixt earth and heaven a breath might waft aside ;
> We breathe one air, beloved, we follow one dear guide :
> Passed in to open vision, out of our mists and rain,
> Thou seest how sorrow blossoms ; how peace is won from pain."

Let this truth that all saints are for one another and are to be made perfect together, stand out in its Biblical simplicity before our faith, unencumbered by any attempts of ours to imagine the modes of this mutual dependence of the living and the dead.

Imagination has indeed its high and holy task in aid of faith ; nor do we fail to feel, even in this life, touches upon our spirits as of unseen powers, and influences upon our hearts whose coming and going no man knows. There may be more points on earth for celestial magnetisms to attract than any science can determine. The stars of heaven are distant, we know not how far; and yet they are present in the motions of this earth, we know not how much. The moon to-night will not be exactly in the spot where our science of the forces balanced in her motions would bid her rise and walk across our sky; and our astronomy, doubting not the ancient order of the heavens, must yet make room in its perfect calculations for the observed fact of some uncomputed celestial influence. There are heavenly facts but half understood in commonest human experience. What sweet influences they who have gone from us still have over us, we cannot tell; what magnetic lines reaching down to human hearts, Moses and Elias, the prophets, and the saints from our own homes may touch from celestial places, passes our knowledge; but this we do know, this at least cannot be gainsaid, that in this earthly life, after every analysis we may make of it, there is found a sacred residuum of spiritual experience, which fails under every test to be reduced wholly to common earthly elements.

Without allowing ourselves to be betrayed into curious and possibly very misleading imaginations of the methods and the manner of the sympathies of all saints, we may take great comfort in the fact of their mutuality and interdependence of existence and destiny, as this fact of the unity of their lives and ours has been partially disclosed in the Scriptures. Does it not revive us like a breath of the Spirit to know this truth of All Saints' day, that we all shall be made perfect together, and none apart; that in God's plan our lives and theirs, whom for a little while we do not see, have been interwoven, and still run on interweaving their threads and colors; that still we are living for them, and they for us in the one kingdom of our Lord; that they in their rest, or in their new activities, are resting, or are ministering, not apart from us, as we in our toils and in our dreams still are living and still are loving not without them; that whatever in higher spheres is transpiring in their lives has also its worth yet to be revealed for us, as our thought and love may have growing worth for them; that whether in some silence of divine light round about them they are becoming holy and radiant with perfect love in their own pure hearts, or whether along some way of God they are now made strong to run with some glad tidings, or whether with the Lord Christ they be permitted with their dear hands to give some added grace and human, homelike touch to the places in his many mansions which He has gone to prepare for us,—still, still, they think, they fly, they rest, they love, not apart from us, and in them and their large happiness the great God thinks also of us; that without us they may not be made perfect in that final unspeakable perfection of all the saints in the last day. And we too—herein is a comfort which we must not suffer any man to take from us—we also are living for them; as the early Church before its Latin corruption did not hesitate in its childlike faith to express in its prayers for the sainted dead this most Christian sense of the mutuality of the believers' lives both here and there. We also are living for our fathers, for our friends who have passed before us, for all the saints, if indeed we are living truly and unselfishly; if we are ripening for their companionships, and becoming strong and pure for celestial thoughts and deeds in the ages of ages.

Men and brethren; you may turn if you will in the scepticism of the understanding from this blessed hope, and rend if you can from your hearts all faith in immortality. You may believe, if indeed in any worthy and unselfish moment you can, that at death we living souls fall into the jaws of eternal darkness; but if we trust as little children the voice of God in our personal consciousness of life, if we are Christians and believe in the Gospel of the resurrection, then why do we belie this hope? why do we belittle and dwarf this mighty faith by our comfortless griefs, by our slowness of heart to understand that we are living with all saints? that in fresh sympathies of heart, and active, joyous interest in each new day of the Son of man, we are living most truly with all saints, living best and with most vital hearts with our own dear saints above, hastening with them the day of the Lord, and becoming ourselves meet to be partakers with them in the final beatitudes of God's grace?

Another lesson from this truth of All Saints' day lies close at hand. I shall have spoken in vain if you do not perceive once more the truth that to be a Christian and to be saved is not merely to become perfect for one's self, and to carry off a crown of glory at the judgment day. It is rather to come to the end of self, and to begin to be a member of a blessed society of spirits. No man is to be saved apart from all the saints. God's law of salvation is a social law, the law of a redeemed society. The social life of the church, therefore, the social unity of the church, is not an adjunct or accessory of the divine constitution of the church; it is an element of the divine idea of the church; it belongs to its essential Christianity. And hence it follows that churches are not revived, and do not grow, if this divine idea of the covenant of believers and the household of faith, is lost sight of, or practically ignored.

Once more, let the lesson come home to us from what I have been trying to say, that individually we cannot grow in grace apart from all saints. There is a beautiful Scripture, the most important clause of which we are too apt to hurry over as we read it: "That ye may be able to comprehend *with all saints* what is the breadth, and length, and depth, and height; and to know the love of Christ, which passeth knowledge, that ye might be filled with all the fullness of God." The condition of knowledge of the love of Christ is that we find it and share it with all saints. Yet this is just what many of us sometimes are not willing to do. We would know the love of Christ with our favorite saints. With all saints, said Paul. You must keep All Saints' day if you would know the length and breadth of the love of Christ. Our theologies must be learned not of our New England divines only, but of all saints. We shall never comprehend the love of Christ, if we sit barred and separated from all saints within our own pews. Pew doors are contrary to Scripture, if they do not open easily to all saints. And still less can any cultured man hope to know God in the capacious solitude of his own intellect. It was Paul, to whom were given personal revelations above measure, who felt the need of learning the love of Christ with all the saints. Yes, those unknown saints, those humble saints, those poor saints, untaught, unlearned, are to be your fellow-helpers to the truth. There are faces among them—I have seen some such—in whose light we may learn more of the secret of the Lord than from any books. Oh, when will we understand that our Christ is the universal Christ? All men come to him. All history is in him. "Behold, the man!" "Behold, the Lamb of God, which taketh away the sin of the world!" Only in universal sympathies can we know the universal Christ. We must come out of ourselves, we must live more with others and in others, we must make All Saints' days in our homes and in our hearts, if we would be learners of the universal Christ, and enter into all the fullness of God.

And finally, for I must close with the half not uttered, let me remind you that to join the Church is to begin to keep All Saints' day before the Lord. It is for any of you to confess that apart from us you cannot be made perfect. It is to act upon your belief in the communion of the saints. It is to come with us and to confess your faith in the Saviour of the world in that simplest form of words, the Apostles' Creed, which more than any other is the creed of the holy catholic Church universal, and henceforth to seek no more alone, and apart, but with all saints to know that divine love which passeth knowledge.

THE END.

www.ingramcontent.com/pod-product-compliance
Lightning Source LLC
Chambersburg PA
CBHW070242230426
43664CB00014B/2388